<u>Note From Author:</u>

*Dear beautiful sister in Christ,
This book won't solve all of your problems.
(It'd certainly be nice if it did!)*

My prayer is that what it will do is bring you in the Presence of God on a daily basis! You may already have a relationship with Him or you may not. You may have opened this and you're currently full of hurt; my prayer is that you'd be filled with hope. You may feel lost; my prayer is that you'd find it in you to seek direction. You may feel unloved; my prayer is that you'd know you are more loved than you can ever fathom. God is Love. You may feel concerned; in His presence you'll find security. You may feel skeptical; read this with an open mind and heart. You may feel you aren't beautiful; through this book you will learn that you've been designed in a special way to do phenomenal things. You are and will be a world changer as you grow to believe you are beautifully made in the image of God
and **He truly loves you**.

Love,

Imani Dunning

Table of Contents

Day 1: **Are Broken Pieces Beautiful?** 3

Day 2: **Where's My Happily Ever After?** 5

Day 3: **Proverbs 31 is tiring!** 7

Day 4: **When Premarital Sex Seems Like a Good Idea** 11

Day 5: **I'm Planning to Stop Planning** 16

Day 6: **When It All Falls Down: Faith** 19

Day 7: **Miscarriage** 22

Day 8: **Breaking Up is Hard To Do** 25

Day 9: **Father, Can You Hear Me?** 27

Day 10: **I Should Be Saved By Now** 30

Day 11: **Serving God to Your Fullest Extent** 32

Day 12: **When I Don't Love Myself** 36

Day 13: **Purpose For Women Of God** 40

Day 14: **Can Men and Women Be Friends? Best Friends?** 44

Day 15: **Lord, Deliver The Ratchet People** 48

Day 16: **The Struggle…Every Month** 51

Day 17: **Beauty** 55

Day 18: **Feeling Unworthy** 60

Day 19: **Modesty In A Naked Society** 64

Day 20: **Tearing Down Those Walls** 68

Day 21: **Why Am I Sowing + Not Reaping?** 72

Day 22: **Dating: God's Way** 75

Day 23: **Clarity + Forgiveness** 82

Day 24: **Peace + Purity** 88

Day 25: **Strength + Patience** 93

Day 26: **Redefining Love + Perspective** 96

Day 27: **Rest + Trust** 101

Day 28: **Listening + Watching** 105

Day 29: **Purpose + Plan** 108

Day 30: **Fear** 111

Day 1: Are broken pieces beautiful?

I daresay they become beautiful when placed in the hands of God.

I may not have been exactly where you are right now, but I've definitely had my fair share of broken pieces. As a matter of fact, I still do. People tell me I'm strong and that I give them hope. They see a finished product yet I see a broken woman held together by grace alone. If that's beautiful to people then to God be the glory--but it is totally and completely His doing.

I believe that the more broken you are, the better. The world says that as women we should suck it up and be strong. We should 'man up', never show our tears, and never show that we're weak. We shouldn't make mistakes because classy women don't slip up. We should dominate every area of life without hiccups.

Apparently I should know how to cook everything, handle a business well, take care of my husband, nurture and appropriately raise our children, look amazing while doing all of this, and have boundless energy because energy will keep me looking youthful. My clothes should be designer, my body should be bigger according to some magazines, smaller according to others, and according to TV I am not nearly enough. According to talk shows, I'll never match up with ideal beauty.

I love to admire heels from a distance... on other women's feet. I will never be a stiletto-wearing woman, and somehow that makes me less beautiful to men, but no less stunning in God's eyes. We face the constant battle between striving to measure up and constantly falling short both in the world, and as Christians. How do we deal with this effectively?

All of this is resolved by spending time at the feet of God, daily. Hand God those broken pieces, questions, hurts, insecurities, doubts, fears, worries, and burdens. A new haircut won't ease your pain. Nor will a new nail color, gossiping about people to friends, shopping the pain away, listening to angry rock songs, or moping alone in your room.

God has a plan for your broken pieces once they're placed in His presence:

James 3:17 But the wisdom that comes from heaven is first of all pure; then peace-loving, considerate, submissive, full of mercy and good fruit, impartial and sincere.

Girl Chat

We've discussed how God can touch and revitalize your broken pieces. Now let's look at your heart and do some self-reflection.

1. When's the last time you prayed about all that you are currently feeling?

2. Do you pray or charge God for what He's done for you?

3. Do you leave it all at His feet and walk away from it or do you pick up your problems and issues again in frustration that He's hasn't fixed them yet? (For example: God help me forgive that person. Then two days later: God I don't see the point in waiting for you to answer this prayer so I'm just going to go do what I want! You're taking too long!)

4. Is there anyone you need to forgive? Tell God and ask for wisdom.

5. Did you forgive yourself for your role in that experience?

6. What do you believe God wants you to do <u>as you wait</u> for Him to heal you? (Hint: It's not pestering Him every two seconds about whether or not He's done *yet*.) If you're not sure, let that be what your next prayers are focused on.

7. Do you trust that God can heal you? If not, it's ok. Pray about that! Tell Him your worries; tell Him you don't see how you'll ever make it out of this one! God is not intimated by your doubt –He knew these questions were coming! Let Him lead you to answers.

Day 2: Where's My Happily Ever After?

What does your happily ever after look like? Does it look like being happily married with kids, in your dream home? Does it look like singing on tour, running your own business, seeing the world, or getting to the top in your career field?

My happily ever after used to be completely summed up by marriage, having my own family, and singing on tour. Yes, I used to think I'd grow up to become a famous singer, go on tour, make millions, and turn my kids into a family band. A girl can dream...right?

In any case, I found God; or rather I realized that He'd been pursuing me. Now while I'd still love for my kids to be able to sing with me and I still desire some of the things I used to desire—those things no longer equate to 'happily ever after' for me. I've come to believe that my beginning and therefore my 'happily ever after' ending is rooted in my God. If I never get any of the desires in my heart, I can find joy because I serve Joy. I can find peace because I serve Peace. I can find hope, help, shelter, and restoration because those are a few of the names and attributes of the Heavenly Father.

Sis, I'm not saying to never have desires or prayers. Just don't *worship* your desires. Don't place them on a higher level in your life than they should be. The more secure your future is, the less you worry about it. If your hope for your future is found in anything outside of God: a relationship, success, acknowledgment etc.—you will surely be disappointed. All things outside of God are quicksand. Give your heart's desires to God and allow God to single handedly create your true happily ever after.

Paul's happily ever after is found in Philippians.
But whatever were gains to me I now consider loss for the sake of Christ. What is more, I consider everything a loss because of the surpassing worth of knowing Christ Jesus my Lord, for whose sake I have lost all things. I consider them garbage, that I may gain Christ and be found in him, not having a righteousness of

my own that comes from the law, but that which is through faith in Christ—the righteousness that comes from God on the basis of faith. I want to know Christ— yes, to know the power of his resurrection and participation in his suffering, becoming like him in his death, and so, somehow, attaining to the resurrection from the dead. (Philippians 3: 7-11)

Girl Chat

We just discovered how even our beautiful fairy tale endings must be laid at the cross. Let's discover yours!

1. What does your happily ever after look like?
2. What do you believe God's happily ever after looks like for you? Why?
3. Do you believe that God will provide the desires of your heart?
4. Do you obsess over this fairy tale? Is it all you can pray, dream, think and smile about?
5. What can you replace your strong desire to pray for your future with? For ex. Prayer for your family, world social issues, your friends, how to grow deeper in relationship with Christ, genocides in the world, sex trafficking victims etc.
6. Look up scriptures on idolatry. Do you idolize your desires? [You can type "idols" into Youversion.com]
7. Find a few women you can trust, share what you're struggling with, and seek accountability! Set up weekly chats/coffee dates/hang-outs to make sure that you can consistently re-direct one another's focus onto God. Or check out the hash-tag #HBGLY on social networks to see if anyone else is looking for accountability! (:

Day 3: Proverbs 31 is tiring!

The Proverbs 31 woman wasn't born that way. She didn't come out of the womb sewing, married, and running a business.

She made a decision to follow God, gain godly character through intimacy with Him, and apply godly truths to her lifestyle. She decided to cast aside her personal preferences, die to her flesh, and *learn how* to be the woman God called her to be.

A Proverbs 31 woman is honest, self-less, transparent, focused, driven, and eager to work. She is never lazy, disrespectful, or inconsiderate. She can be found serving the needs of her household, her business, or the poor and needy. She is solely about her Father's business.

She never complains, she gives God the glory for *everything*, she handles life and people with grace, and she smiles at the storms ahead. She prepares for the storms ahead. She seeks counsel, insight, godly teaching, and continually grows in her relationship with God. Her <u>intimacy with her King</u> *transfers over* into the affairs of her household and business. She's come to understand that the key to life is an intimate and consistent relationship with the One who created life.

The Proverbs 31 woman made and continues to make sacrifices that many women wouldn't necessarily make. Character development is found in the little things day by day that "don't seem like a big deal." It's found in obeying everything God has called you to do: forgive everyone, love everyone, change your attitude towards that person, spend time with God daily, read your Word, get in a community of Christian women and anything else He's called you to. Not spending time with Him may not seem like a big deal, "it was only once this week", but how can you expect to be a woman of godly character without consulting God? You won't become the woman God called you to be without Him, and without passing the tests you face.

The Proverbs 31 woman *finds pleasure* in serving. She finds pleasure in all of her roles and I gather she had to find pleasure in her role as a single woman of God, first. She mastered the art of finding contentment and joy in each season. She takes on a lot as we can see from everything she does—yet she sees it all as service that she's happy to provide. How often does someone have to ask you to do the dishes? How often do you jump over a pile of your clothes to get into bed? Is your brush in the kitchen and your other shoe in the living room? Is the only meal you know how to cook easy Mac? If any of these are descriptions of you don't beat yourself up about it, change it.

Whether marriage is in your future or not, you and your guests deserve to enter a clean area when you all enter your home. Clean—not shoes and clothes piled high and hidden in the closet—actually clean. You should have balanced meals for the sake of your health, and bank account. Ordering out can lead to spending thousands yearly on meals you could have taken some time to make at home. Get a cookbook, ask a good cook for lessons, search for recipes online, or get creative and make healthy versions of your favorite foods. I absolutely have a huge obsession with hamburgers. So when I crave one, I make veggie burgers from scratch and I might add Daiya cheese for some extra flavor. You don't have to be vegetarian to eat healthy, just conscious of your food intake.

When you and your friends hang out don't be afraid to be the oddball that says "no" to McDonalds. They may look at you in a weird way but you're prepared to respect your body and make healthier decisions. This can mean bringing lunch/dinner from home or bringing food from a healthier option and meeting them there later. This is what I was referring to when I said a Proverbs 31 woman makes decisions other women wouldn't necessarily make.

Let's look at her. Proverbs 31: 10-12, 15-18, 20, 25-27 (emphasis added in bold)

A wife of noble character who can find? She is **worth far more than rubies**. Her husband has **full confidence in her and lacks nothing of value**. She brings him **good, not harm, all the days of her life**. She gets up **while it is still night; she** provides food for her family and portions for her female servants. She considers a field and **buys it; out of her earnings she plants a vineyard. She sets about her work vigorously**; her arms are strong for her tasks. She sees that **her trading is profitable and her lamp does not go out at night**. She **opens her arms to the poor and extends her hands to the needy**. She is clothes with **strength and dignity; she can laugh at the days to come**. She **speaks with wisdom, and faithful instruction is on her tongue**. She watches over the affairs of her household and does **not eat the bread of idleness.**

Girl Chat

We just read about how the Proverbs 31 woman is constantly serving and selfless. Let's take a look in the mirror.

1. Instead of hating or envying the Proverbs 31 woman, ask God to help you become like her! What things do you already do, that make you a woman of noble character?

2. Proverbs 31:30 says Charm is deceptive, and beauty is fleeting; but a woman who fears the LORD is to be praised. What does this verse mean to you?

3. Proverbs 31:26 says she speaks with wisdom. This requires being slow to speak and measuring the outcome of what she's thinking before she says it. What are the circumstances and who are the people that you believe cause you to want to blow up immediately? Who is that person who always knows how to push your buttons? Do you believe it is important to speak with wisdom and make sure every word is wrapped in grace before it leaves your mouth?

4. She brings her husband good and no harm all the days of her life according to verse 12. What do you need to change in order to ensure you bring everyone you come in contact with good and no harm all the days of your life? What can you do to better serve your enemies?

5. How can you set about pursuing the dreams and goals God has placed in your heart, now?

6. Do you know any women who you feel embody aspects (or the whole) of Proverbs 31 really well? What do you do to get around them and allow them to pour into you?

7. How do you react when storms come? Do you roll around in agony praying to be delivered, or do you stand up and face them knowing they are for your good and to help you glorify God better?

Day 4: When Premarital Sex Seems Like a Good Idea

I've been there! Your heart is racing, your body has run out of excuses, your mind is going blank, and your Spirit is crying out. You may see flashes of old sermons, old teachings and verses in the Holy Spirit's attempt to remind you who you say you serve.

You may feel sick as you head to their house or they head to yours, you may feel dizzy, and you may feel like that dream you had the other night is getting too real. Far from your mind is the young girl you just mentored, the songs you sang on Sunday, or the worship filled lifestyle you claim to have. Maybe right now you're having flashbacks of the last time you gave in. Or the first time you gave in. It was bad but not that bad, right? You may have felt guilt, which you quickly shrugged off and now you're right back at the threshold. You're at the edge of the cliff, hanging in the balance between giving in to what your flesh wants and holding onto the God you know deserves your heart, body, mind and soul.

I remember praying earnestly for God to give me direction, the secret formula, or to come possess me to stop my body from making bad decisions. I asked how to stop the dreams, the urges, the actions that led to worse, the decisions I'd come to realize were <u>not mistakes</u> but *choices* over the God I claimed to love.

John 14:15 says If you love me, you will keep my commands. I love to sing the praises of the Lord, I love to worship, I love to dance for God in church, I love to pray, I love getting to know my God but everything I just said is a lie if my life isn't ruled by obedience to His Word. The Bible describes the praises of those without love, like the clanging of cymbals. 1 Corinthians 13:1 says *If I speak in the tongues of men or of angels, but do not have love, I am only a resounding gong or a clanging cymbal.* My praises sound like 5 years olds banging on pots when I shout out to God all the while **knowing I'm intentionally sinning** against Him.

I believe in the power of God's grace and mercy. I believe it swarms in and crashes into us, in the midst of our praise. I believe it knocks down our walls and releases us from strongholds. I believe grace covers and that God draws near to us, because the bible says so. I believe that God's mercies are new daily because the Bible says so. However, I also believe that we have an obligation to *demonstrate* our love and commitment to God by obeying Him. I believe He desires for us to be unafraid of strictly living by His commands.

I know that this is sometimes thwarted by Christians who take the Bible out of context, bash others for not living how "they think they should live", and millions of stereotypes about militant-like religious people who do nothing, refrain from wearing black, and refuse to have fun for fear that 'the devil will somehow seep in'. When I say strict living, I am referring to the ever increasing abandonment of our flesh. I don't believe that for most of us, we'll abandon everything that is like us and take on *everything* that is of God—in one sitting. Then God's work would be complete in an instant and we'd have nothing else to learn. I believe that aspects of our flesh can certainly be immediately transformed and killed, with a strong conviction to never turn back.

Scriptures never really worked for me in the past, the way that they do now. When my boyfriend was in front of me, my mind blanked of all the good reasons I should walk away. I mean, he's hot... why would I walk away from that? I needed to get burned, hurt, broken, abandoned, violated, mistreated, and cheated on by those I thought would carry my heart in order for me to begin to see that all the darkness in the world couldn't possibly bring a happy ending outside of God. For me, and I've noticed for many others, we tend to have this superwoman—"I can do it all—mentality. We tend to believe we are exempt from the repercussions that others have faced before us. We tend to believe we'll have the story of "doing everything wrong yet receiving all God has to offer in the end." Don't cheat yourself out of a godly and fully satisfying blessing for garbage. Doing things outside of the context God designed it for, is like stuffing your body and mind with poison and garbage. It's not for you and there's a reason God detests it!

Speaking of feeling exempt from repercussions, let us look at Ezekiel 23. I briefly read a few verses in the Day 4 video but I'd like to go a little deeper here.

In Ezekiel 23, Ezekiel shares a word that the Lord shared with him. God tells the story of the cities Samaria and Jerusalem in an interesting way. God changes Samaria's name to Oholah and makes her the older sister, and changes Jerusalem's name to Oholibah and makes her the younger sister. The entire chapter refers to both nations as two adulterous sisters, and He explains how the two sisters became prostitutes in Egypt and engaged in prostitution since their youth.

I would really encourage you to sit down with a pen and paper and read the whole chapter. I encourage you to pray beforehand for God to reveal to you how, if at all, it relates to your life. I will just highlight a few verses that impacted me.

Ezekiel 23:4-8 (emphasis added in bold)

The older was named Oholah, and her sister was Oholibah. **They were mine** *and gave birth to sons and daughters. Oholah is Samaria, and Oholibah is Jerusalem. Oholah engaged in prostitution* **while she was still mine**; *and* **she lusted after her lovers**, *the Assyrians—warriors clothed in blue, governors and commanders,* **all of them handsome young men**, *and mounted horsemen.* **She gave herself as a prostitute** *to all the elite of the Assyrians and* **defiled herself with all the idols of everyone she lusted after.** *She* **did not give up the prostitution** *she began in Egypt, when* **during her youth** *men slept with her, caressed her virgin bosom and* **poured out their lust on her.**

Ezekiel 23:10, 11-13, 40, 41, 43 (emphasis added in bold)

They stripped her naked, *took away her sons and daughters and* **killed her with the sword.** *She became a byword among women and* **punishment was inflicted on her. Her sister Oholibah saw this, yet in her lust and prostitution she was more depraved than her sister.** *She too lusted after the Assyrians—governors and commanders, warriors in full dress, mounted horsemen, all handsome young men.*

I saw that she too defiled herself; both of them went the same way. *They even sent messengers for men who came from far away, and when they arrived* ***you bathed yourself for them, applied eye makeup and put on your jewelry.*** *You sat on an elegant couch, with a table spread before it on which* ***you had placed the incense and olive oil that belonged to me.***

Sis, let me tell you sin only leaves you open, vulnerable, naked, and without hope. Sin leaves you isolated, broken in the worst way, in pain, and so far from God who longs for you—His precious daughter. I know sis, I've been there. It feels like getting on a roller coaster, enjoying the surge of fear mixed with pleasure, but suddenly you're thrown out of your seat. You flail your arms as you fly through the air, you scream but no one hears you, and you crash into the ground as your world soon follows. In the midst of it all, you hear and see many others still on the ride--still going. The sound of your own breath echoes and you feel like walls are closing in on you even though you're outside. The ones you were on the ride with are all gone. Now it's just you sitting in your mess by yourself. You look up at the Father you'd long ago abandoned; He looks the same...just so much farther away. Then you're wrecked because it's been so long and you don't know how long it'll take for you to reach Him. He spared your life but in the midst of all your broken bones, you wonder why He bothered.

The reason I love those verses is because all I see is God's broken heart. I see Him cringing as His daughter who He lovingly and repeatedly refers to as **His own**, lets yet another idol destroy her life. All I feel is God's tears as He remembers His perfect son on that cross. He was whipped, mocked, beaten, scorned, yelled at, spit on, imprisoned, and ultimately hung on a cross for *you*. I just feel God's heart breaking all the more as He wonders why that perfect sacrifice just isn't enough for His daughters. Why isn't His grace enough? Why isn't His perfect love enough? Why isn't His provision enough? Why is it that His <u>perfect plan, perfect track record, and perfect timing</u> are not enough for us, sisters? Why are we so impatient, chasing after the wind, men who'll never love us the way Jesus does, men who don't desire to submit to God, and then surprised when we crash straight into a brick wall? That's all sin is: a cold, lonely, condemning dead end.

Girl Chat

I truly pray that God revealed some key things to you through this chapter. Let's chat!

1. How many times did you squirm and/or cry during this Day 4 devotional? Come on, I can't be the only one! Did God speak to you?

2. I implore you to take a few moments and praise God for your life. You may be ashamed of your past, but God isn't. He saved you because He knew one day you'd yearn for Him more than all of your former idols. Do you believe that you're forgiven? Do you forgive yourself?

3. What changes do you feel you need to make in your friendships, relationships, daily walk as a result of your convictions? Go make them now. It's worth it!

4. Do you know anyone struggling with this right now? Pray for them earnestly and daily.

5. What has God revealed to you about himself in this chapter?

6. Do you believe that you are capable of rising above sexual sins? Do you know that God longs to help you? Often we may view Him as fuming with anger at our mistakes—God has at least just as much love for you as He does disappointment in your unholy decisions. If not more.

7. Do you find yourself "preparing to sin"? Do you find yourself getting dressed up to see someone you shouldn't see, daydreaming about the guy God told you to let go of months ago, or perhaps texting or calling the guy who's more into *you* than God? Challenge yourself to prepare to serve God with your whole heart, mind, and body.

Day 5: I'm Planning To Stop Planning

I've been planning to stop planning for years now. I read my old journal entry the other day from 2011 in which I wrote that I have given up on planning, orchestrating, and running. I wrote that God would no longer have me fighting with Him as He pushes me into unknown territory. I think that was a beautiful desire and I believed God could bless that prayer, but I thought it'd happen instantly. I thought I could write it down, and it would just happen to be so.

I've learned that there are layers hidden behind our stacks of plans. To clarify, I don't mean to say that you should never have a goal or dream. It is important for you map things out to the best of your ability. However, there is something seriously wrong if whenever God tells you to *let go* of those plans, you fight Him. There's something wrong if God reveals His plan to you and you can't accept it because you think your plans are better. The layers behind those kinds of plans can cripple your destiny. You can't get where God wants you to be without following Him.

It's worth it to be willing to replace each of your plans with God's plans. We need to learn to trust that our desires are woven into God's plan. If you give up your plan, <u>you're not giving up the opportunity to be blessed</u>. You're showing God you trust Him, and that the blessing and His timing are truly perfect.

I believe that it is important to find a balance between reaching the goals you've set and operating under God's guidance. He trusts us to get things done, yet it is important to hold your decisions up to His Word. For example, when I went to college, I knew instantly that I wanted to finish as soon as possible. I felt it would be important for me to take various measures in order to achieve this goal. I don't recall actually hearing God say "Imani, go finish school in 3 years." However, I do believe that I was graced to do this and every time I came up against an obstacle, I experienced a miracle. For me, that was an indication that I was going the right direction. I stepped out, and God met me there every single time.

It is a huge struggle for women who have a tendency to plan too much, to believe that everything is can run smoothly without their input. After we obey, we are so ready for the next step! We can't wait to hit the ground running again. We tend to struggle with waiting periods where God hasn't given us any further instructions because there's nothing to plan, nothing to focus on, and nothing to fill the void. This place is exactly where God wants us. It's exactly where God wants you: the place where your hands are tied and you have a huge void that nothing and no one can fill. Then and only then, will you allow God to fill it as He alone was meant to.

Ultimately, the best way to measure your plans up to God's is to ask Him, listen to your conscience, hold your thoughts up to the Word of God, through fellowship at church, seek godly counsel, and listen for the voice of God where ever you are. God will reveal when you should walk and when you should wait. He'll redirect you when you make a wrong move, and often warn you before you do. Often we overanalyze things yet we know right from wrong. You know if you shouldn't go somewhere, or be with that person...sometimes we look to God for a sign that disproves our conscience. Be honest with yourself and make the decision that will most glorify God.

Proverbs 16: 1-4, 9 says:

To humans belong the plans of the heart, but from the Lord comes the proper answer of the tongue. All a person's ways seem pure to them, but motives are weighed by the Lord. Commit to the Lord whatever you do and he will establish your plans. The Lord works out everything to its proper end—even the wicked for a day of disaster. In their hearts humans plan their course, but the Lord establishes their steps.

Girl Chat
It is critical to partner with God to achieve His perfect will for your life. Let's explore ways to do that effectively.

1. Is there anything you're planning right now that you feel God wants you to let go of? (i.e. finances, jobs, marriage, ministry, relationships)

2. Do you believe that God's design truly is the best plan for your life?

3. What do you fear will happen if you don't plan everything out? (i.e. you'll look silly, God will fail, your life will fall apart)

4. What does Habakkuk 1:5 mean to you right now?

5. Which area of your life is the hardest to trust God with? Why do you think that is?

6. Write down or record as many of God's promises as you can remember. Do you repeat these or meditate on these daily? (If not, I'd encourage you to start! It's so inspiring.)

7. When is the last time you sought prayer for this area of your life? Do you believe you need someone to pray in agreement with you?

Day 6: When it all falls down: Faith

Faith is the substance of things hoped for yet unseen. In other words, you strive to confidently believe in and for things you have yet to see. In addition, you live from that faith daily. You make your decisions or you patiently wait--while standing on that faith!

Luke 8:13 says, and those upon the rock [are the people] who, when they hear [the Word], receive and welcome it with joy; but these have no root. They believe for a while, and in time of trial and temptation fall away (withdraw and stand aloof).

Numbers 23:19 says, God is not man, that he should lie, or a son of man, that he should change his mind. Has he said, and will he not do it? Or has he spoken, and will he not fulfill it?

Often we have no problem believing that God will eventually help us. We begin to struggle when God hasn't done what we wanted Him to, in the time frame we expected. Had God done what we wanted immediately, we wouldn't worry or fret about our circumstances. It's when He requires that we grow in maturity before blessing us (which is often), where we run into trouble.

I can recall being really frustrated with God because I felt He was taking entirely too long. I'd just like to encourage anyone reading this that the harder the trials; the bigger the breakthrough. Certain things can seem cliché when they are overused; however I have experienced this first hand. I can recall being incredibly stressed out about how bills would get paid, and in due time they were paid. They weren't paid because I managed to make anything happen; in fact often my hands were completely tied. I have experienced being unemployed, hopeless, and I felt really alone, yet God kept me in His grace.

At first repeating verses like Philippians 4:6-8 wasn't helpful. It felt like chanting foreign things that held no ground in my life. It was the epitome of speaking things as though they were, and to be frank it was frustrating. It bothered me that I couldn't see them taking place. It really bothered me to see everyone around me getting blessed, employed, favored, and graced. I didn't like the season I was in because I felt ignored by God. God brought the following resources to mind that helped me endure and grow to trust Him more.

Deuteronomy 5:29 states: Would that they might always be of such a mind to fear me and to keep all my commandments! Then they and their descendants would prosper forever.

"Lord, high and holy, meek and lowly, Thou hast brought me to the valley of vision, where I live in the depths but see Thee in the heights; hemmed in by mountains of sin I behold Thy glory. Let me learn by paradox that the way down is the way up, that to be low is to be high, that the broken heart is the healed heart, that the contrite spirit is the rejoicing spirit, that the repenting soul is the victorious soul, that to have nothing is to possess all, that to bear the cross is to wear the crown, that to give is to receive, that the valley is the place of vision. Lord, in the daytime stars can be seen from the deepest wells, and the deeper the wells the brighter Thy stars shine; let me find Thy light in my darkness, Thy life in my death, Thy joy in my sorrow, Thy grace in my sin, Thy riches in my poverty, Thy glory in my valley." –"The Valley of Vision," A Puritan Prayer.

Girl Chat
We are called to deal with life differently than others do. We are called to leave behind impulse and choose to wait on the guidance of our God.

1. What is your first response when you feel like you're under pressure?
2. How have your responses and perspectives changed since you began your relationship with God?
3. What are your go-to scriptures when life is difficult? Do you have them readily available for when tough times hit?

4. Do you have a small-group community that meets regularly outside of church for prayer and fellowship? It may be helpful for you to join or start one so you can have somewhere to be openly transparent.

5. What does Philippians 2:13-16 mean to you? How does it relate to your current circumstance or perspective?

6. Are there times you can recall where you chose to hold on in spite of difficulty, and everything worked out?

7. Does God's perfect track record encourage and inspire you to trust Him all the more for provision?

Day 7: Miscarriage

One of my favorite resources for Christian women is todayschristianwoman.com which is a branch of the organization Christianity Today. Women share their testimonies of how they've personally overcome various things and miscarriage is one of the topics addressed.

I've never personally experienced miscarriage but what I've come to understand is we have to tie ourselves to timeless truth. Truth is a person and that person is Jesus. We have to allow Him to join us in our grief, sorrow, pain, misunderstanding, anger, frustration, and anything else we may feel. We have to let Him into our messy lives and into our overwhelming circumstances. He can calm the storms and the winds of this life, and when we run from Him in anger; we run away from the only one who can cure our hurts.

Unfortunately being a good person, serving God with all your heart, donating to the poor, or doing good deeds doesn't make you exempt from life's hurdles. Rather, a relationship with God serves as an anchor in the storms of life and a promise for eternal life. God can handle the weight of your world, the weight of your grief, your raw honesty, your dark thoughts, your groans when you lack the words to pray, your agony, your stress, your questions, and all that you've been bearing.

I would just like to encourage you to bring all of your feelings to God. Let Him know your hopes, dreams and desires. Let Him know how disappointed you are and don't be ashamed to cry out repeatedly. Let Him know all the thoughts that are swarming in your mind. I know sometimes we're taught to pray eloquently with certain formats, but I believe God works with us. I believe that He will allow His peace to invade your sorrows as you cry out to Him. I believe that His hands will cup around your heart as you cry. I believe that His healing power is in no way limited and that nothing you do can separate you from His love. I believe that God is waiting to bear your burdens and that He isn't intimidated by your anger or any of the feelings you may be struggling with.

These are biblical truths about the character and heart of our God. We must hold onto these when life gets overwhelming, shocking, and seems unfair. There are times when your heart is broken in so many pieces, that you hardly recognize yourself. It is possible to feel nothing but pain in the morning when you wake up because your life weighs so heavy on your heart. I'd just like to encourage you: God hasn't changed, He hasn't left, He's still on the throne, He's still for you, He's still with you, and as crazy as it may sound He understands the murmurings of your heart.

I believe the hardest part about this walk is **that there is no quick-fix**. There is no pill, or 5 step program that will just miraculously make it all better. You have to make a decision to follow God and stick with Him when it feels good and when it doesn't. You have to make up your mind that you will place all of your life, heart, hope, mind, and soul in God's hands to do with it what He will. You cannot avoid difficulty and strife in this lifetime, but He has promised to give you a life in which you are blessed and He is glorified. It just requires that you leave what the blessings and glorifying God look like, up to God. We will spend the duration of our lives slowly warming up to that release of control over our lives and dying to our flesh.

Psalm 34:18-19 says: The Lord is near to the brokenhearted and saves the crushed in spirit. Many are the afflictions of the righteous, but the Lord delivers him out of them all.

Romans 8:18 says: For I consider that the sufferings of this present time are not worth comparing with the glory that is to be revealed to us.

Jeremiah 29:11 says: For I know the plans I have for you, declares the Lord, plans for welfare and not for evil, to give you a future and a hope.

Psalm 147:3 says: He heals the broken hearted and binds up their wounds.

Girl Chat

It is important for us to rest in God's healing power. His love covers everything and everyone.

1. Have you or anyone you know experienced this? Did you/they cope with or without seeking God's help?

2. Both men and women have to deal with this if both parties are actively involved. How has your church directly or indirectly provided support?

3. What do you believe are common myths concerning miscarriages?

4. Do you blame yourself? If so, take your reasons to God in prayer and lay them at the altar.

5. Have you spoken to anyone about your past? If so, I'd encourage you to pray about a leader or prayer buddy that you can be vulnerable with.

6. What does Psalms 119:73-75 mean to you?

7. Is God your source for the love, affection, guidance, and security that you need?

Day 8: Breaking Up is Hard to Do

"Human history is the long terrible story of man trying to find something other than God which will make him happy."- C.S. Lewis

Although break ups hurt, they can sometimes be the best thing for your purpose. It may take that person leaving, or you leaving to really catapult you to where you need to be. You need to focus on the purposes God has placed in your heart and if that person was in the way—it was only a matter of time before they'd be removed.

We have all heard the stories of people who break up and then get back together. They have a testimony of how God used the time apart to strengthen them and strengthen their love for one another. I do believe that for some, that is God's desire for their lives.

It's important to realize that your story will not look exactly like everyone else's. God closes doors that He wants closed, and keeps select doors open. It is important to give God full reign and control over your life and heart. He formed, crafted, and knew you intimately before you were a thought in your parents' minds. The truth is God knows all the plans that He has for you and as we read earlier, they are plans to prosper you not harm you and give you a hope and a future.

Allow God to present you with the blessings He's designed for you, in the perfect timing. Allow God to withhold what He knows you don't need, from you. Don't fight Him and don't play tug of war with that person. If God tells you to let them go, let them go. Realize God is helping you from the knowledge that a man of God wants a woman for her mystery. He wants to earn her heart, her trust, and her time.

Think of it this way: if you give it all over to God and He wants to restore your relationship, you'll be in a better place to move forward when God gives you two the green light. If you give it all over to God and God chooses not to restore the relationship, you'll find yourself so deeply involved in the will of God, it eventually won't matter. God will meet you where you are, restore you, heal you, and bless you according to his riches and glory in heaven. Psalm 19:1 says *the heavens declare the glory of God; the skies proclaim the work of his hands.* Believe that the Creator of the world has a perfect plan for you.

Girl Chat

People easily find themselves holding onto the world tighter than their hold on God if they aren't careful. God only has us let go of people so we can receive better.

1. What do you believe to be some common misconceptions concerning break-ups?

2. If this is a continual cycle in your life, do you believe there are any changes you need to make? What are they?

3. Have you submitted this to God? He has the power to heal, restore, and revitalize your passion to serve Him all the more, in spite of life's circumstances!

4. Have you prayed for God to release you from soul ties? There are both emotional and physical soul ties.

5. Do you have a mentor who can walk with you through this process?

6. Are you operating in forgiveness towards yourself and that person?

7. How can you dedicate more of your life and heart to God this year?

Day 9: Father, Can You Hear Me?

God wanted you to achieve His purpose and plan for your life, long before you knew He had one. He wants His plans for you to come to pass more than you do. He wouldn't have placed gifts, talents, and dreams in your heart if He didn't want you to partner with Him to see all of them happen. This world desperately needs what's inside of you. Thus, of course God hears you, longs to direct you, and longs to breathe on your dormant gifts and circumstances to bring His perfect will to pass.

God placed specific things inside of you that you add your own value and personality to. No one can fill the role He crafted you to fill, the way that you can. You were placed in your family, in your friendships, in your school, in your job, in your neighborhood, and in your circumstances because all of it is meant to mold you into just the type of vessel God desires to use. A vessel that is broken, available, and ready to run hand in hand with God. Is that you?

We struggle with whether or not God hears us when we feel neglected. There are times when we pray and don't receive an answer, we believe for something and the opposite happens, or perhaps we pray for something and it seems like everyone around gets that but us. It can seem like you got the short end of the stick—where God answers your friends' and strangers' prayers before He answers yours.

I'd like to encourage you not to be envious of the blessings of others. Instead celebrate with them, cover them in prayer, and pray for God to pull pride out of you. Pride says "I'm entitled to my blessing now," instead of truly laying your cares at the altar and believing God will work everything out in perfect timing. Humility says "God have your way! I have my preferences but I believe your will is better than mine so I've resolved to wait no matter how long it takes." I believe God appreciates the latter more than the former. Humility is the response of a child that loves God *more* than they love His gifts.

When thoughts swarm and cause me to worry, I re-calibrate myself to the will of God. The way that Jesus managed to be both present in this world and focused on heavenly things, is that He was finely tuned to the will of God. Though he was God in the flesh, we see Him constantly in prayer, fasting, and seeking the face and direction of His Father. There was an astonishing level of intimacy between Jesus and God throughout the duration of His time on this Earth. Thus, I resolve to do as Jesus did and pray about my role that I may be about my Father's business as He was.

Each and every time I do this, I am filled with energy and I am presented with a project to focus on. This project allows me to participate in the plans of God for my life and distracts me from what isn't happening. It is a brilliant opportunity to be so focused on serving God that what I prayed for begins to matter to me less. If all you do during the day is think and complain about what God hasn't done, it will lead to a miserable experience. As mentioned prior, I believe it is God's will that we are constantly in the business of serving, not tapping our feet and timing God as though He has any obligation whatsoever to do things in <u>our timeframe</u>. I guarantee that just trying to live out the following scripture alone, will keep you busy.

Philippians 4:8-9 says Finally, brothers, and sisters, whatever is true, whatever is noble, whatever is right, whatever is pure, whatever is lovely, whatever is admirable—if anything is excellent or praiseworthy—think about such things. Whatever you have learned or received or heard from me, or seen in me—put it into practice. And the God of peace will be with you.

Girl Chat
Prayer is the communion of our hearts with the heart of our Creator.

1. How does God normally speak to you?

2. Have you ever felt like He failed or disappointed you? If so, why is that?

3. What resources do you use to combat your doubts and negative thoughts?

4. What time of day do you most struggle with doubt/worries? Knowing that you can expect these things around that time, what can you do to best prepare yourself?

5. What does Philippians 2:2-4 mean to you?

6. Do you use prayer or various methods to manipulate God into doing what you want?

7. If you are good at serving God with humility, do you share your insights with women who may need help around you?

Day 10: I Should Be Saved By Now

"Remember that sometimes not getting what you want is a wonderful stroke of luck." – Dalai Lama

I know that I constantly struggled with believing that I should be further along in my walk than I felt I was. Sometimes we read the Bible and cover our faces because we are so far removed from the faith and reverence we read about.

I believe the tension comes because humans are all about the present and God is all about the process. We tend to continually want everything now. We want deliverance, a significant other, a spouse, a promotion, a full-time ministry, a dog, a house, a car, healing, provision, wisdom, an answer from God, and a perfect relationship with God all right now. We don't see why we shouldn't have it now after all of our hard work, dedication, blood, sweat, and tears …but God does.

Our lives become the battlefield for a huge tug of war challenge between our flesh and godly living. Our flesh is comfortable; godly living challenges us. Our flesh separates us from God; godly living draws us closer. It is easy to give in to our flesh; it is a daily struggle to live solely the way God has commanded us to live. Thus we have moments where we regret every word we just said; and the next day we manage to humbly serve for 15 hours without complaint.

Whatever age you are, you find yourself facing the same battle. Now, as you strengthen your resolve to follow God whole-heartedly, various things become easier and different sins lose their grip on you. It never fails that you're presented with a bigger challenge than ever before or a bigger loss than ever before. God stretches your faith by using storms, trials, and difficulty. If you want to grow in your faith and become closer to God, expect tests that increasingly cause you to rely less on yourself and depend on God alone.

1 John 4:20 (NABRE) says: *If anyone says, "I love God," but hates his brother, he is a liar; for whoever does not love a brother whom he has seen cannot love God whom he has not seen.*

Mark 14:38 says: *Watch and pray so that you will not fall into temptation. The spirit is willing, but the flesh is weak.*

Hebrews 12:1-3 says: *Therefore, since we are surrounded by such a great cloud of witnesses, let us throw off everything that hinders and the sin that so easily entangles. And let us run with perseverance the race marked out for us, fixing our eyes on Jesus, the pioneer and perfecter of faith. For the joy set before him he endured the cross, scorning its shame and sat down at the right hand of the throne of God. Consider him who endured such opposition from sinners, so that you will not grow weary and lose heart.*

Girl Chat

It is challenging but worth it to give everything up to follow God. Let's discuss!

1. How have you changed since last year?
2. Do you have a community of friends that can pour into your spiritual life?
3. Do you feel intimidated by God's expectations of His children?
4. How can you apply Mark 14:38 to your life?
5. Are there any revelations/promises that you reflect on during difficult seasons? If so, when's the last time you shared one with someone struggling?
6. How has your perspective on what walking with God means, changed over time?
7. How can you apply Hebrews 12:1-3 to your life?

Day 11: Serving God to Your Fullest Extent

One question women constantly ask me is how they can serve God better. They recount a few of their most recent sins, tests, and difficulties to give me a clue as to why they asked the question. They hope that I will give them a solution that will solve this issue for good. I imagine that people see the hand of God on my life and want to know the "secret." The secret has been made public through the Word of God. To serve God better requires intimacy.

It requires a relationship where you work hard to make God your number one priority. You have to learn to identify Him as your Master, Creator, leader, and best friend. Often when people think of a master or leader, they think of someone who is untouchable. They think of someone who they are vaguely aware of but that their role concerning their master is simply to obey. When people think of a master or leader, they may view them as a CEO of sorts where the leader is responsible for delegating and the employee is responsible for making those things happen.

God has a perfect design which He discloses to His children. God planned everything out including your name, hometown, favorite color, and the number of countries that would be on Earth before the foundation of the world. God orchestrates your day to day life and that of everyone you know. He orchestrates the lives of everyone on Earth whether or not they believe in Him. Nothing has ever happened that God himself has not allowed. No solution, help, invention or event has ever occurred without the knowledge and approval of God. God releases the very knowledge that men seek. God is sovereign and He reigns over all the Earth. The lack of submission in the world does not and will not change the fact that God sits on the throne. God has given us free will that we might have the opportunity to *desire* to serve Him. How amazing is it that it **matters to God that you choose to love Him** though He has the power to *make* the world love and fear Him? Unfortunately, so much of the world revolts in spite of His acts of grace towards us as seen in 1 John 2:15-16.

Though in all of His grandeur, we reverence His name with fear and trembling, God longs to be more than your Master. God longs to be more than your leader and more than someone you quietly follow. He wants to give you more than instruction. He longs to offer you so much more than His lordship. God wants to demonstrate His perfect love for you in a deeper way than you've ever felt love. More than reverence out of fear, God desires your love and devotion. He created you to love you! He desires to be your very best friend and to have an intimate relationship with you. 1 John 4:16 says *And so we know and rely on the love God has for us. God is love. Whoever lives in love lives in God, and God in them.* In addition 1 John 4:18 says *There is no fear in love. But perfect love drives out fear, because fear has to do with punishment. The one who fears is not made perfect in love.*

Dear sister in Christ, I'd like to further extend to you an invitation that God has already given you. This invitation is to take His hand in marriage. Devote yourself to Him as you would your husband, submit to God's instruction, spend every moment of free-time with Him as you would with anyone you love, listen for the voice of God, remain alert to the things He is orchestrating around you and love Him with all your heart. No moment is a mistake and no moment lacks divine purpose. When you love, you will be drawn to submit. When you spend time with God and you desire His way over your own, you will be drawn to love Him more. When you tire of doing things your own way, getting hurt by the same type of men, getting frustrated by the same people, hating everything about your job, stressing out about finals, feeling lonely, and feeling unworthy—that is when you will be open to an all-encompassing relationship with God.

When will enough be enough? When will you accept love—the perfect way—so that you now have a standard to hold your man to? When will you accept what God believes about you so that when doubt seeps in, you can confidently say you <u>love</u> the woman in the mirror? When will God's perfect track-record and never-ending pursuit of your heart, finally convince you that God is enough? God has graced you enough times, He's woken you up enough times, He's rescued you enough times, He's answered enough prayers, and He's performed miracles enough times to deserve your unconditional devotion. Don't you think so? Romans 12:11-12 instructs us to: *Never be lacking in zeal, but keep your spiritual fervor, serving the Lord. Be joyful in hope, patient in affliction, faithful in prayer.*

When you pursue and fall in love with the King of Kings—that is when you will serve better. You will serve more, you will devote all of yourself, you will obey quicker, you will follow without needing to understand, you will be fearless as you adopt His character and find your sustenance in the presence of the Lord. I challenge you to stop doing what you've been doing. If it hasn't been working, it's time for new methods. I challenge you to really open up to God—ask Him what you should do to get closer to Him. Then, *wait for the answer!* Don't ask God a question, wait five minutes, then say you "knew it wasn't going to work." You've spent 10-20+ years doing everything your own way and **God waited for you.** Wait on God and trust that He will respond. Remember that He longs for your heart and devotion so He will be sure to help you if that's your heart's desire. It may take longer than you think it should. It may not look how you expect it to, but when you give your heart to God you place your timer and your running shoes in His hands as well. Stop running from God and stop checking the time. He created time, why would you use it against Him? Trust that God is capable of making His own will (which is intimacy with His children) come to pass and that He will guide you as to what your role is in making this happen.

Romans 12:2 says *Do not conform to the patterns of this world, but be transformed by the renewing of your mind. Then you will be able to test and approve what God's will is—his good, pleasing and perfect will.*

Girl Chat
The grace of God runs deeper than we can imagine just so we can be sure we'll never fall out of it.

1. How can you apply Romans 12:2 to your life today?

2. In what areas of your life do you struggle with trusting God?

3. Do you read Christian books on the areas where you struggle? (I recommend Crazy Love by Francis Chan and Grace by Max Lucado)

4. Do you tend to wait on God or do you get impatient quickly?

5. Do you believe that God's grace is sufficient for you?

6. How can you rearrange your schedule daily to make spending time with God a priority? (I suggest you get a partner to do this with you).

7. Do you live your life as though you need God for everything or are your interactions with Him limited to saying grace before meals or prayers with that "religious family member" during the holidays?

Day 12: When I Don't Love Myself

It breaks my heart to hear that people struggle with this. Not that I believe anything is wrong with them, but because I know how much joy and peace they miss out on. It turns out that's a lesson I'm still learning today! I'm learning it is a <u>constant</u> process of renewing my mind, choosing God over every thought, choosing God over every desire, choosing to love with the love of Christ instead of lust filled obsession, and saying "No" to the things and people God says "No" to.

Life is a process of trusting God in a new way for the same thing every day.

Your perspective isn't wide enough to see all the amazing things that make up what a gem you truly are. When we're born our scope is limited, then experiences and people limit it all the more. Imagine our confidence as an inflated balloon. As children, often we feel we can accomplish anything, until the first person tells us otherwise. That balloon deflates over time and after a while the air isn't going in as fast as it's coming out. You can probably understand how that feels. People compliment you or you do a great job on an assignment, but it doesn't quite pick you up as fast as negativity puts you down.

Your perspective of yourself doesn't have enough depth or context to withstand the hurt and negativity of this world. You need God's perspective because when you believe His, it means you believe the Truth about yourself.

I said to myself, "God will bring into judgment both the righteous and the wicked, for there will be a time for every activity, a time to judge every deed." (Ecclesiastes 3:17)

I lift up my eyes to the mountain—where does my help come from? My help comes from the Lord, the Maker of heaven and earth. He will not let your foot slip—he who watches over you will not slumber; indeed, he who watches over Israel will neither slumber nor sleep. The Lord watches over you—the Lord is your shade at your right hand; the sun will not harm you by day, not the moon by night. The Lord will keep you from all harm—he will watch over your life; the Lord will watch over your coming and going both now and forevermore. (Psalm 121:1-8)

When you don't love yourself, it is because you're viewing yourself from the wrong perspective. You're viewing and judging all of your broken pieces. You're feeling that they make you unworthy, as opposed to a better vessel. God can use broken vessels; in fact, I personally believe they're the easiest for Him to use. When you're broken you're more likely to be obedient, desperate, honest, transparent, and follow Him wherever He leads. When you're broken, you recognize that God is your only option. Often my prayers have been "Lord; I'm relying on you to live. If you don't feed me, pay my bills, or provide for me I simply will not make it." As a matter of fact, my bank account was just in the negative the other day and God provided more than enough to take care of that situation. If He did it for all those people in the Bible, and if He can do it for me, He can and will do it for you.

Ask God to show you what came to mind when He was creating you. Ask Him to show you the traits He loves about you and teach you to love them too. Ask Him for help and be honest about those places where you could use improvement. Surround yourself with people who build you up and speak godly things over you. It's counterproductive to work on your self-esteem and hang out with so-called friends who tease and tear you down all the time. Read what the Word says about what you may struggle with. It may be beauty, personality, feeling socially awkward, weary because of your past, paranoia about your future or many other things. I believe one of the most comforting messages of the Gospel and the Bible is that people's humanness and flaws didn't put them out of the running in the Great Commission. In fact, it qualified them!

The things you think make you inadequate, less than someone else, or incapable of completing a task God has called you to; are the very things God wants to use for His glory. Even in doing this series, I've had a few thoughts about whether or not I'm qualified, pure enough, familiar enough with scriptures etc. God revealed to me that I was called for this and thus God would stand in the gap if need be. He wanted me to learn and understand that my past, my flaws, and my habits don't disqualify me from doing work that honors Him. They don't disqualify me from anything, but grace encourages me to refrain from living my old life. God saved, covered, and is delivering me daily from wrong perspectives and pulling my ugly ways out of my heart. Thus I write this not as a squeaky clean angel oozing with righteousness but as a sinner who's devoted her life to daily encounters with the Creator. You can do that as well! It's not about what you've done, the stretch marks, or the scars (inside or out), it's about who holds your heart. I challenge you to hand it over to the one who created it. He's waiting for you and He loves you with a perfect love.

"To be loved but not known is comforting but superficial. To be known and not loved is our greatest fear. But to be fully known and truly loved is, well, a lot like being loved by God."-Timothy Keller

Let's resolve to give God our broken pieces and our incorrect perspectives, in exchange for the Truth.

Girl Chat

The only way to love right is to love the way that God does. He'll help you; just draw near to Him.

1. Do you love yourself?
2. Do you rank your love for yourself based on how many mistakes you've made or based on comparison at all?
3. How has God's love for you changed the way you view yourself?
4. Are your friends your support system? Do they cover you in prayer, lift you up, listen to you, fight for you, appreciate you, and love you in a healthy way?
5. Do you have a spiritual circle of people who intercede on your behalf?

6. How much time do you spend studying scriptures that pertain to things you struggle with?

7. How many Christian books have you read pertaining to the areas you struggle with?

Day 13: Purpose for Women of God

I pray that you'd not only read this book for help with various topics but that ultimately it would drive you to God's feet. I pray each chapter drives you into prayer, deeper into His presence, stirs up more passion in you for Him, and creates a new hunger for His Word and His presence. After all, I'm sharing what God has placed on my heart, yet it tends to be specific for my life. I'd love to hear how God speaks to you as you read this, and more importantly the Word, on a daily basis.

I believe everyone on Earth is created for the same foundational purpose; we are just equipped with different skills, talents, backgrounds, and gifts to accomplish it. First, I'll explain what the purpose is and then how this relates to you.

I believe we were created for God, by God, to glorify Him. I believe that God purposed for every person on Earth to glorify Him with their lives. Now we all have free-will and of course billions of people have chosen not to follow God, yet that doesn't change that on the most basic level they were created for Him. I believe one's decision to *refuse* their purpose doesn't negate the fact that it *is* their purpose. They just choose not to live from it. The fact that people don't believe in God doesn't change the fact that **God exists**, reveals himself to people daily, and performs miracles around the world every second. It doesn't change what is true; it merely means they miss out on intimacy with Him and the grace that is capable of covering their sin.

What the Bible says about those who choose to live outside of the Lordship of God is found in many places but let's look at Romans. Bold text is my added emphasis; these things aren't highlighted in the Bible.

Romans 1:18-20 says: The wrath of God is being revealed from heaven against all the godlessness and wickedness of people, who suppress the truth by their wickedness, since what may be known about God is plain to them, because God has made it plain to them. For since the creation of the world **God's invisible** qualities—his eternal power and divine nature—have been clearly seen, being understood from what has been made**, so that **people are without excuse**.

Romans 1:21 says: For although they knew God, **they neither glorified him as God nor gave thanks to him**, but their thinking became futile and their foolish hearts were darkened.

Our purpose is referenced here: To those who by persistence in doing good seek glory, honor and immortality, he will give eternal life (Romans 2:7)

We are able to carry out this purpose because of what Jesus did for us. Romans 3:23-26 says: *For all have sinned and fall short of the glory of God, and all are justified freely by his grace through the redemption that came by Christ Jesus. God presented Christ as a sacrifice of atonement, through the shedding of his blood—to be received by faith. He did this to demonstrate his righteousness, because in his forbearance he had left the sins committed beforehand unpunished—he did it to demonstrate his righteousness at the present time,* ***so as to be just and the one who justifies*** *those who have faith in Jesus.*

Essentially, God allowed Jesus to come that he might restore our opportunity for intimate relationship with God. Our intimate relationship with God allows us to ask questions, receive divine revelation, pray, and spend time with Him. As we do these things, God teaches us how to be more loving, kind, forgiving, honest, fair, long-suffering, patient, and ultimately more like Him. Though this is critical and the most important aspect of life (receiving salvation and beginning sanctification through Jesus), there's more to your purpose.

You have gifts, skills, talents, perspectives, and so much more within you. You have your own special way of relating to, understanding, and interacting with people. Maybe you play instruments, dance, sing, draw, act, inspire, persuade, write, translate, encourage, serve or do something really well. God gave you those talents and your personality. Everything about you was *designed* to demonstrate God's existence and glory. Your smile, your joy, your impact when you use your talents, your influence, your past, your present, your goals, your great work ethic etc. are all tied into God's purpose and plan for your life.

Does this mean you have to work in a Christian school, organization, lounge and teach/sing about *solely* Christian topics in order to walk in your purpose? I believe you should follow your own convictions. There are Christians in every field with the light of God shining through them, then there are people who claim to believe in God but their lives don't demonstrate this. The goal is to receive direction from God and go do what He says. If He says to go into the music industry, then go. *But bring God in there with you; don't conform to what everyone else is doing.* Wherever you end up: live a life filled with grace, purpose, passion, forgiveness, kindness, but above all submission to God. There should be something different about <u>you</u> in your workplace, school, home, organization or wherever you are. You should live in such a way that people can say, "Wow, she is one of the most patient people I know." "She's so quick to forgive." "Her joy fills up the room." "Her peace is contagious." "When everyone else is stressing out, she manages to remain calm."

If people don't say these things about you, it's perfectly fine. We live for an audience of One, sisters! The point is when you live in a way that glorifies God; it *impacts the environment you're in*. When you do that; you are walking in your purpose.

Girl Chat
We have millions of messages sent to us through various media channels. Let's discuss how to set and keep our dial and focus on one channel—God's.

1. Do you know your purpose(s)?
2. Do you do what you're passionate about, for the glory of God?
3. How have you felt limited by society or people as it relates to going for your dreams?
4. What gifts/talents do you have?

5. What are you doing now and is that in line with your passions?

6. How can you begin something now that you enjoy? If you already do, how can you help other women do the same?

7. What are some challenges you face? What scriptures can you turn to in order combat these?

Day 14: Can Men and Women Be Friends? Best friends?

This is a touchy topic for so many people because they have strong opinions. I really like Chadia Mathurin's take on it in her blog post "Being a Virgin Isn't Enough." Here's an excerpt: *"I asked myself is God were to allow me to meet my husband today, would I be in a place of emotional integrity that he is worthy of? How many men am I emotionally attached to? How many "friends" do I need to redefine myself with? ... There is a compliment and then there is a deliberate stroking of the ego. I understand that it is not my job to make a man who is not my husband or intended husband feel like he is Superman. You affirm a man too much, he either becomes attached if he's not averse to the idea of a relationship or runs if he is averse."*

There are different kinds of "friends." Or rather I should say there are various levels of depth in relationships period. There are the "hi and bye" interactions, where you say hi to people that you see around but that is the extent of both your relationship and interactions. There are the people that you hang out with once in a while—the only time you communicate is about when you'll see one another next. There are the people you identify as friends who you speak to multiple times a week. Then there are your best friends—who you speak to all the time, you are in nearly constant communication, you literally do life together. With these people, rarely does anything go on in their lives that you're unaware of and vice versa.

With men, these levels are a bit more loaded. For example, if there are guys you only say hi and bye to—it may be linked to a lack of attraction or lack of similarities that would warrant deeper conversation. For example, I tend to have "hi and bye" interactions with 98% of the guys I know, not because they are unattractive but neither of us have felt the need to have a longer conversation or spend time together. Then there are the men who I talk to every now and then, we might share prayer requests, pray in a group setting, and talk about surface issues every now and then. Or we might grab coffee to discuss our business ventures etc. These interactions denote commonalities more than they denote friendship. Then there are guy friends--there are very few people in this category. We don't venture into making deep emotional attachments but we have actual conversations. These may be people from school or an organization where we've known one another for a good amount of time. Then there are best friends—honestly I have one guy best friend. I strive not to pour my heart out so intimately to men that I can't ensure will protect it, reciprocate, and stick around. Personally, I feel that level of intimacy and openness should be bound with a relationship (and with reservation if unmarried).

I used to be the type of girl who unloaded very heavy emotions and experiences on men immediately. I saw *every guy* as my potential "best friend" so I would share my hurts, frustrations, joys, and I would speak about everything with them. I would do this in hopes that if I let it all out, they would help me filter through all of these emotions and my issues. I essentially wanted them to partner with me to deal with my life. There was only one problem. I had way too many "partners" trying to filter through things that were entirely too personal. No man should be burdened with venturing through my mess, unless he's in it for the long haul. Otherwise they are dealing with issues that I should give over to God, and often the thought would arise "why take it to God when I have all these men available to sift through my needs with me?"

Song of Songs 8:4 says Daughters or Jerusalem, I charge you: do not arouse or awaken love until it so desires. David Guzik's Commentary explains this scripture as the following: **In terms of relationship it means, "Let our love progress and grow until it is matured and fruitful, making a genuinely pleasing relationship-*don't let us go too fast."* In terms of passion it means, "Don't let us start until we can go all the way." What is this warning? That love is so sacred a thing that it must not be trifled with. It is not to be sought. It stirs and awakens of itself. To trifle with the capacity for it, is to destroy that very capacity.**

I would admonish you to take your heart's desires, pains, troubles and everything within you to God in prayer. Let Him be the partner who sorts through everything with you. If God gives you the green light to allow someone else on the journey alongside you then, go ahead. Just don't take it upon yourself to bring men who haven't been approved by God, into your mess with you. It could lead to emotional attachments and feelings arising without the proper foundation. When I poured out my deepest thoughts on these men, often either I liked them (and felt they should reciprocate because I'd given so much), or vice versa. Sometimes I poured out so much and didn't want to be with them, nor was I attracted to them but the increase in our intimacy led them to believe that I'd have a mutual attraction to them which simply wasn't the case. This led to strained friendships and broken relationships that resulted in broken hearts, misguided perspectives, and aches in the voids that were unsuccessfully filled by the other person.

Let God determine who should be relegated to distance in your life. Guard your heart in your friendships. Don't tie yourself so tightly to men who will one day tie themselves to someone else, leaving you all with a mess of strings, threads, and confusion. Tie yourself to God who can form you into a woman of God who's ready for a man of God (if you desire to be married), and use <u>one</u> string to tie you to the man He's equipped for you. *One string, one bond, one covenant…forever.*

Girl Chat
Obey the conviction in your heart—regardless of whether or not it is your preference.

1. What is your personal conviction concerning this?
2. Have your friendships ever become murky or problematic?
3. If God were to tell you to let go of a friend right now, would you?
4. How do you feel your friendships have helped you to grow?
5. Do you have any friendships with men that you now believe are perhaps 'too deep' to be healthy right now?

6. Does God speak to you about any of your current interactions/habits? For example: flirting, spending excessive amounts of time with people, compliments, or sharing too much personal information.

7. How did the scripture and the explanations above, affect and/or convict you?

Day 15: Lord, Deliver the Ratchet People

Often we pray incessantly for people to get delivered from their horrible ways. We pray for the people who have hurt us, those who've hurt people we know, those who yell at strangers, people who annoy us, people who anger us, and people who accuse. Sometimes it is out of genuine, heartfelt concern but other times our prayers are laced with distaste for the person and their actions.

Sometimes our prayers have a "clicking of the tongue and an eye roll" thrown in there to demonstrate just how crazy that person is. When we pray for deliverance for that person, we wish that they'd finally "get sane." This will be the year they finally get their lives together…finally they'll stop driving us crazy, right?

The problem with these types of prayers is that they paint the wrong picture. They paint a picture of you in all of your glorious humility, taking your time out to pray for the people who get on your nerves. You tell yourself that you're doing them a favor and you're doing something holy because you're doing what the Bible says by praying for your enemies. But God looks at your heart. He knows if you're praying for them to see them come into the fullness of life in Christ, or if you're praying for them to feed your ego and pride.

Pride says: I'm going to pray for them so they'll leave me alone. Pride says: I'm going to pray for them and let them know I'm praying for them so they'll see just how crazy I think they are. Pride says: Lord, deliver the ratchet people.

An accurate painting would show them drenched in sin, in need of a helping hand. It would feature you also drenched in sin but holding on to the hand of God. You're holding on to God's hand, as well as this person's hand, drawing their hands to one another. Essentially, you are using your life as a vessel to get that person into the presence of God, knowing that they will find all they've been looking for there. You're on your face before God praying that the person would be protected, covered, loved, and encouraged to find God so they can feel the joy that you feel. Do you see the difference?

Humility says: Lord I'm just as broken as they are. But by grace you've saved me and by grace you can save them. Humility says: God please help me use every opportunity to demonstrate your love to these people. Humility says: Lord please kill all the perspectives I have that don't match your perspective because they hinder me from doing your will with a clean heart. Humility says: Lord, please deliver them *as you continue* to deliver me.

In the same way, count yourselves dead to sin but alive to God in Christ Jesus. Therefore do not let sin reign in your mortal body so that you obey its evil desires. Do not offer any part of yourself to sin as an instrument of wickedness, but rather offer yourselves to God as those who have been brought from death to life; and offer every part of yourself to him as an instrument of righteousness. For sin shall no longer be your master, because you are not under the law, but under grace. (Romans 6:11-14)

Love must be sincere. Hate what is evil; cling to what is good. Be devoted to one another in love. Honor one another above yourselves. Share with the Lord's people who are in need. Practice hospitality. Bless those who persecute you; bless and do not curse. Live in harmony with one another. Do not be proud, but be willing to associate with people of low position. Do not be conceited. If it is possible, as far as it depends on you, live at peace with everyone. (Romans 12:9-10, 13-14, 16, 18)

Girl Chat
Perspective changes everything; including our behavior.

1. How long does it take you to forgive offensive people?//
2. Do you believe they deserve a negative response because they made the first offense?
3. How do you deal with people who pester you repeatedly about things? Particularly—people who have a lot of advice on how you should live your life etc.

4. What did you learn/gain from the scriptures above?

5. What changes should you make to your language and perspective as a result?

6. Is there anyone you need to forgive?

7. Have you ever taken the time to ask God how He sees the person you despise or feel uncomfortable around? (I'd encourage you to try it!)

Day 16: The Struggle... Every Month

I've heard quite a few women discuss their struggles with purity and self-control each month around their menstrual cycle. It's as though they are perfectly fine for 20 days or so, but during their cycle they become women ruled by emotions and hormones. Our bodies are so amazing; if you think about it. Each month, it prepares for you to have a baby. For those of us who are not looking to have a baby this month, this process can seem rather pointless, but the amount of detail that goes into this process is stunning. Your brain receives various signals, your body reacts to those signals, and your body produces everything you need in order to be prepared. Then it alerts you if you're missing anything (for example, if you need more salt or fluids). All of this is in preparation for the baby that could possibly appear this month. And this intricate process happens 12 times a year! I can't quite wrap my mind around how creative God is, it truly leaves me speechless.

In any case I'd like to address some of the things that I hear. I've heard about lust issues, pride issues, over-emotional behavior, anger issues, and so much more. It's as though our inner monster is largely contained but each month it breaks free and makes a run for it. I'd just like to share that our God is bigger and stronger than all of your urges, fantasies, and impulses. Though your flesh is weak, your spirit is willing and if you'll let God intercept all of those messages you can see great results.

I believe the problems in all these areas come because **we indulge in them**. We feed the monster instead of casting it down. We call that guy instead of calling on God. We daydream instead of meditating on scriptures. We give in instead of fighting. Then we want to "repent" each month because "we're so sorry about what the monster did."

It wasn't a monster. That was all you sis.

For me, I used to get overly physical during my cycle. I just wanted to hold hands, cuddle, and feel closer. I suppose it makes sense if my body is preparing for a baby. Well the problem is it caused me to push limits and play with fire. It caused me to do things I wouldn't normally do, and continually blame it on the monster. However, in reality the monster is my scapegoat—our scapegoat—for a lack of self-control. We blame her when we go too far or if things get out of hand. She bought the donuts! She grabbed him there! She dialed that number! She made me do it. Sis, let's be honest that was your hand, those were your thoughts, and those were your choices. Thoughts, ideas, and suggestions come but you have to choose between whether you'll cling to the Father or let that monster out. Whichever you choose becomes your <u>default reaction.</u>

Purity has to be more than a thought, more than guilt, and more than fear of others finding out...it has to be a deeply rooted conviction. Where does this deeply rooted conviction come from? Well for many people it comes from getting burned repeatedly, unfortunately. *Conviction doesn't have to come from making all of the wrong decisions.*

Let's take a look at a few of God's precious promises.

Fear not, for I am with you; be not dismayed, for I am your God; I will strengthen you, I will help you, I will uphold you with my righteous right hand. (Isaiah 41:10)

Blessed is the man who remains steadfast under trial, for when he has stood the test he will receive the crown of life, which God has promised to those who love him. (James 1:12)

I have blotted out, as a thick cloud, thy transgressions, and, as a cloud, thy sins: return to me for I have redeemed thee. (Isaiah 44:22)

Let's look at the following example.

[Moses] regarded disgrace for the sake of Christ as of greater value than the treasures of Egypt, because he was looking ahead to his reward. By faith he left

Egypt, not fearing the king's anger; *he persevered because he saw him who is invisible.* (Hebrews 11:26-27)

Let's look at a few warnings.

For where you have envy and selfish ambition, there you find disorder and every practice. (James 3:16)

Therefore subject yourselves to God. But resist the devil, and he will flee from you. Draw near to God, and he will draw near to you. Cleanse your hands, you sinners, and purify your hearts, you double-minded! (James 4:7-8 LEB)

And have you completely forgotten this word of encouragement that addresses you as a father addresses his son? It says, "My son, do not make light of the Lord's discipline, and do not lose heart when he rebukes you, because the Lord disciplines the one he loves, and he chastens everyone he accepts as his son. Endure hardship as discipline; God is treating you as his children. For what children are not disciplined by their father? No discipline seems pleasant at the time, but painful. Later on, however, it produces a harvest of righteousness and peace for those who have been trained by it. Therefore, strengthen your feeble arms and weak knees. (Hebrews 12:5-7, 11-12)

Hold onto instruction; do not let it go; guard it well, for it is your life. Do not set foot on the path of the wicked or walk in the way of evildoers. Avoid it, do not travel on it; turn from it and go on your way. Above all else, guard your heart, for everything you do flows from it. Give careful thought to the paths for your feet and be steadfast in all your ways. (Proverbs 4:13-15, 23, 26)

You have to make a decision as to whether God will have all of you or none at all. He's given His all to you so will you reciprocate this sacrifice in exchange for abundant life you can't begin to imagine?

Girl Chat

1. Do you find your struggles with various things increase around the time of your cycle?

2. What do you do to combat your heightened levels of estrogen?

3. If what you currently do is ineffective, do you reach out to others who you deem exemplary to learn how you too can live in consistent purity?

4. What did God speak to you as you were reading this? Write it down, if you heard anything.

5. Have you confessed and sought accountability with a sister in Christ?

6. Are there any experiences in the past that could've led to your current lack of self-control in this area?

7. Better behavior comes from better habits. Better habits come from better thoughts. What does Philippians 4:8 mean to you?

Day 17: Beauty

"Pour yourself a drink, put on some lipstick, and pull yourself together." - Elizabeth Taylor

The world defines beauty as the quote above. Somehow beauty has become miniskirts, short dresses, just the right amount of cleavage showing, tight bodies, long hair, make-up, heels, and one's ability to wipe their broken heart away by applying lipstick and alcohol to their wounds. It seems year after year, women push the boundaries further in an effort to publicly "embrace their sexuality". Men don't have to wonder how 'so and so' looks naked because she's shown enough of everything on the red carpet, in music videos, or on movies. Porn was once taboo and distasteful, but now movies across many genres have become soft-porn. People are becoming more and more desensitized: <u>viewing sin as humor</u> and unashamed perversion as modern culture. It's absolutely disgusting and it leaves women feeling uglier and more inadequate than ever.

How am I supposed to teach my daughters about their inherent worth and beauty if everywhere they turn, they see messages that scream otherwise? How am I supposed to tell my sisters in Christ that their natural hair, natural skin tone, natural body weight, natural body shape, and natural personality are **perfect in the sight of God** when they feel they still need a way to get a man's attention? It may get increasingly difficult to get the message across but I will continue to share it and the Holy Spirit will continue to embed it into hearts daily.

Since when are you not beautiful unless you look like her? Write that lie on a piece of paper, throw it in the trash, and never say it again. **You are the daughter of the one true King.**

He didn't make you to be like anyone else and He yearned for you. The world was full of people and He kept crafting until He made you! You matter. Your worth is found in Christ's hands.

My heart breaks for all the many ways we are told we're not good enough, pretty enough, thin enough, thick enough, and tall enough. Then we suddenly have to learn to believe God when He says we are good enough. I hear "I'm not enough" multiple times a day and *people don't have to say it for me to hear it.* It's a soundtrack continually playing in my mind. But let's turn the dial up on the volume of our Father's voice so that His love and truth will drown out every voice and lie that says otherwise.

I despised my body well into high school! Everything was too skinny, long, and awkward to me. I wondered why my skin wasn't lighter, why I had stretch marks, why I had so many bruises, and why my shoe size was an 8/9 in a world where 6/7 is normal for a woman. In actuality, a 6-7 shoe size is average yet *in my mind I turned* average *to* **normal**. Not fitting the mold made me feel ugly and it made me believe I couldn't possibly have anything to offer the world, let alone a man. I wondered why my fingers were long and skinny, why my legs were longer than my torso, and why I was so skinny (as everyone including family and friends just loved to point out). I resented my breast and butt size and it seemed as though everyone else did too!

I was always cute and little <u>instead</u> of beautiful and bold unlike the young ladies around me. I was inevitably friend-zoned while my thicker friends were vied over by boys. I was the girl you eat lunch with (in a group setting) whereas all the girls around me were pestered for their number and a Saturday date night!

I couldn't understand why I was cursed with size 0 jeans and no money to at least make them designer in high school! I resented everything about me (including my eye size). I caused myself so much suffering by constantly comparing myself with women who didn't even know I existed. With every woman who walked by, I just went down the list. Her hair is longer than mine, straighter than mine, a more interesting color than mine, and more versatile than mine. Her butt is bigger than mine, her chest is bigger than mine, her nails are always done, her face is prettier than mine, her sneakers always look nicer than mine, her phone is better than mine, and her style is better. Eventually these negative thoughts turned to questions and me shaking my head at myself in the mirror. Why don't I have a beauty mark on my face like her? Why do I have so many pimples? Why do I have stretch marks <u>when I haven't even given birth</u>!? Why are my feet so big if I'm short—what on Earth do I need big feet for then? Why am I short? Why can't I have bigger breasts? Why do I have so many scars all over my body? The list went on and on. As I mentioned earlier, I went through this list every single time someone walked by me. As you can imagine, I was in a constant state of distress.

Beauty, for me, meant everything about a person. The clothes, body, hair, how much attention they got and personality. It truly bothered me that in my opinion, I had none of that. Besides being good at school, I didn't feel like there was anything else to me. Even with family members telling me otherwise, it didn't quite stick. After all, I figured family members are supposed to encourage you, in addition, you also kind of look like them so of course they'll say you look great. Then after a while, men were more than happy to attempt to fill all these voids I had and I didn't see how that could be a problem. I was missing something. Actually, I was missing everything. I was missing appreciation, love, support, consistency, intimacy, confidence, self-worth, and truth. We discovered in previous chapters that truth is a person. Truth is God. I was missing God and didn't know it.

If you feel any of the ways I just mentioned, or something similar, I'm here to tell you: you're missing God. You may use various things to fill those voids, but they'll all fall short sis! God placed a desire for himself and for eternity deep within you. As you get older, you notice the void and you ache over the fact that it isn't filled. Filling it with parties, drinking, too many relationships, shallow friendships, and meaningless activity is like pouring water into a glass with a gaping hole in it. Your void has a specific shape. The shape is the hand of God and nothing will make you whole but the hand of God on your life.

(Bold emphasis is my own.)
He has made everything beautiful in its time. He has also **set eternity in the human heart**; yet no one can fathom what God has done from beginning to end.

(Ecclesiastes 3:11)

Let us not look to the things of this world (all of which will pass away) for security, hope, comfort, acceptance, or peace. Peace is found in Jesus and when we try to self-medicate using all the wrong things, we choose the world over God. We choose to sedate ourselves to the point of numbness rather than surrender to God who embodies the cure. It makes no sense, yet we find ourselves doing it or thinking of doing it often. What do that party, person, and drink all have in common? The fact that they're all temporary! Choose God over it all, let Him heal you, guide you, let Him direct your paths, and let God show you how to live the life Jesus died for you to have.

They exchanged the truth about God for a lie, and worshiped and served created things rather than the Creator—who is forever praised. Amen. (Romans 1:25)

It is my prayer that you and I will be able to confidently say the scripture below, about ourselves.

At one time we too were foolish, disobedient, deceived and enslaved by all kinds of passions and pleasures. We lived in malice and envy, being hated and hating one another. But when the kindness and love of God our Savior appeared, he saved us, not because of the righteous things we had done, but because of His mercy. He saved us through the washing of rebirth and renewal by the Holy Spirit, whom he poured out on us generously through Jesus Christ our Savior, so that, having been justified by his graces, we might become heirs having the hope of eternal life. (Titus 3:3-7)

Girl Chat

Beauty needs to be defined by your Creator.

1. Do you believe that you are beautiful?

2. How have other people/situations influenced the way that you view yourself?

3. What are some biblical truths that you can remind yourself of, when doubt comes?

4. What came to mind for you while reading the scriptures above?

5. How can you encourage a sister (or a few) that you know are struggling in this area?

6. What thoughts and beliefs do you struggle with concerning your own body image?

7. When is the last time you looked at yourself in the mirror and told yourself that you are beautiful? Do it as soon as you can.

Day 18: Feeling Unworthy

It seems like it is easier to feel unworthy, sad, and upset than it is to maintain joy. We have to pursue joy while negativity pursues us!

I do believe we live in a fallen world which can contribute to our struggles while on Earth. However, I believe that our own ignorance plays a huge part in struggling with these feelings. I don't mean this in a negative way. The definition of ignorance is lack of knowledge or information.

We are ignorant of the effect that experiences have on us emotionally and spiritually. We assume that thoughts and emotions are all we suffer from. However, each situation touches us and runs deeper than the surface. I'll discuss this further in a future book but let's look at what our experiences do to us. This revelation absolutely blew my mind.

Experiences produce seeds in us that take root in various places and remain hidden. The hurtful words they said, the hurtful things they did, and the ways you devalued yourself, are all seeds that are within your soul somewhere. It doesn't mean that you haven't been healed or that you haven't forgiven everyone you need to forgive; just that you haven't taken the roots out.

We fall into the belief that everything that happens is an *isolated event* that doesn't relate to things in the future. For this reason, we tell ourselves it's ok to date anyone we want using no discernment, we do what we want, we say what we want, we watch what we want, and take full advantage of our free-will. After all God gave it to us, to be fully used without restraint right? Wrong.

My point is there are things that either others ascribed to you or things you ascribed to yourself that resulted in your current feelings. For example, I was teased at school, I dated mean guys, and I scrutinized myself daily for various things. Although years have passed, those feelings of being unworthy still pop up at times. Why? I forgave, I've moved on, and I'm nice to myself but those experiences still have their roots within me. I never took the time to address them because I assumed they weren't there.

I addressed and dug up the roots with God's help by praying specifically for His help in that department. I asked God to reveal the origin of all these feelings so that I could face them. Then I prayed for direction and discernment for how to dismantle the roots' hold on me. I prayed for the strength to rebuke thoughts that didn't glorify God or uplift me. I prayed for the discernment to notice when comments/thoughts had underlying malice to them. For example, I would spend at least 30 minutes scrutinizing my body and staring at it, noticing all the things I dislike about it. I wouldn't tell myself that my body was ugly, however my intent was to scrutinize not celebrate.

God asked me why I felt the need to sit and scrutinize His handiwork knowing full well that He was satisfied with my body. To which I had no response...so I stopped looking. He told me to start being grateful and that the love and acceptance would come. He also gave me fashion and cleaning tips. I didn't even know God knew or cared about my fashion! He addressed the character traits I disliked and revealed so many ugly areas of my heart. There are blogs available detailing a few of these revelations on imaniserves.com.

In any case, I began to praise God for everything about myself. I praised Him for my body and particularly the areas I'd previously detested. I praised Him for things like my fingers—though I didn't understand why He formed them the way He did, they were sufficient at helping me carry out His will. If they're good enough for Him, they're good enough for me. I used them to write this book and I chose gratitude for them and everything else that makes up who I am. Once I chose praise and gratitude, I noticed my attitude change over time.

I can't say that I absolutely adore everything about myself, but I completely **accept** all of me. I resolved not to have higher standards for how I should look than **my God who created me**. I realized I wasn't proving anything to anyone and I was only hurting myself. I was tearing away at my self-esteem among other things and low self-esteem prevented me from starting many things because I felt I wasn't good enough.

So the Lord God caused the man to fall into a deep sleep; and while he was sleeping, he took one of the man's ribs and then closed up the place with flesh. Then the Lord God made a woman from the rib he had taken out of the man, and he brought her to the man. (Genesis 2:21-22)

You have searched me, Lord, and you know me. For you created my inmost being; you knit me together in my mother's womb. I praise you for I am fearfully and wonderfully made; your works are wonderful, I know that full well. (Psalm 139:1, 13-14)

If you struggle with image or self-worth, I encourage you to read psalm 139 in its eternity and pray the verses 1-18 over your own life! It's such a precious perspective on how intimate God knows and interacts with us, His children.

But when you ask, you must believe and not doubt, because the one who doubts is like a wave of the sea, blown and tossed by the wind. (James 1:6)

As a prisoner for the Lord, then, I urge you to live a life worthy of the calling you have received. (Ephesians 4:1)

I encourage you to pray earnestly for the state of your heart. Pray boldly and full of confidence in God's power and capability to change your perspective. He is able, He is worthy, He is glorious, He is all-powerful, He is all-knowing, and He desires for you to be whole sis! He is willing to work miracles in you but it's your responsibility to let controlling and negative habits go and let God in.

Girl Chat

Affirmations are really important. They dictate the way you feel about yourself and life.

1. What does 2 Corinthians 10:4-5 mean to you? How can you apply it to your life?

2. What does God say to affirm you when you're down? Have you written these affirmations somewhere to serve as reminders?

3. How often do you spend time intentionally seeking God and His voice?

4. Have you ever read and prayed Psalm 139:23-24 during your quiet time?

5. Do you meditate on encouraging scriptures throughout the day, daily?

6. Is there anyone you talk to, anything you listen to, anything you watch, anything you read that may contribute to you feeling unworthy? (For example, certain people's social networks, magazines, degrading music, movies with degrading women's roles, old conversations/arguments between you and your ex, or friends that tear you down.)

7. Have you improved and gained confidence in any way over the past year? Have your perspectives in some areas, worsened over the past year? How can you do what worked more often and challenge yourself to stop doing what led to problems?

Day 19: Modesty in a Naked Society

Women, at least every woman I know, tend to care a lot. We tend to care more than we should, more than men, more than our teachers, more than certain friends, more than our parents, more than our siblings etc. If you are someone with a big heart, then you know what I mean. You love more than the average person, you generally follow-up with people often, and you pray for others without having to be asked.

The problem is that it is entirely too easy (and too popular) for us to care about all of the wrong things. We care so much, we pour out so much, and we give so much of ourselves to the wrong people for the wrong reasons. I don't know if it is because society has taught us to seek a "happily ever after" in a world gone wrong, or seek love before Christ, a high before consistency, relationship before maturity but whatever it is; is killing morals all over the world.

My heart is burdened greatly for the woman who vies for a man's attention at a club every week, the woman who believes if she wears less he'll love her more, the woman who knows she's been failing at replacing God with men in the past, yet continues to try. She's never single, she never covers her body, and she desires physical temporary intimacy over the perfect love God offers. She knows all that man, club, party, drink and impulsive decision will lead to is disappointment. She feels the nudge in her Spirit to stay home, she feels the nudge to stay away from him, she feels the nudge to let go of her friends that don't help build her up and propel her toward her dreams but somehow—like so many women—she feels she'll be the exception. She'll be the one to get God's design for her life, by doing whatever she wants. The truth is she won't and neither will you and I—God's design requires that you allow Him to order your steps.

Therefore, with minds that are alert and fully sober, set your hope on the grace to be brought to you when Jesus Christ is revealed at his coming. As obedient children, do not conform to the evil desires you had when you lived in ignorance.

But just as he who called you is holy, so be holy in all you do; for it is written: "Be holy, because I am holy." (1 Peter 1:13-16)

Now that you have purified yourselves by obeying the truth so that you have sincere love for each other, love one another deeply, from the heart. For you have been born again, not of perishable seed, but of imperishable, through the living and enduring word of God. (1 Peter 1:22-23)

Like newborn babies, crave pure spiritual milk, so that by it you may grow up in your salvation, now that you have tasted that the Lord is good. You also, like living stones, are being built into a spiritual house to be a holy priesthood, offering spiritual sacrifices acceptable to God through Jesus Christ. But you are a chosen people, a royal priesthood, a holy nation, God's special possession, that you may declare the praises of him who called you out of darkness into his wonderful light. Once you were not a people, but now you are the people of God; once you had not received mercy, but now you have received mercy. (1 Peter 2: 2, 5, 9-10)

...When they see the purity and reverence of your lives. Your beauty should not come from outward adornment, such as elaborate hairstyles and the wearing of gold jewelry or fine clothes. Rather it should be that of your inner self, the unfading beauty of a gentle and quiet spirit, which is of great worth in God's sight. (1 Peter 3:2-4)

Therefore, since Christ suffered in his body, arm yourselves also with the same attitude, because whoever suffers in the body is done with sin. As a result, they do not live the rest of their earthly lives for evil human desires, but rather for the will of God. For you have spent enough time in the past doing what pagans choose to do—living in debauchery, lust, drunkenness, orgies, carousing and detestable idolatry. They are surprised that you do not join them in their reckless, wild living, and they head abuse on you. But they will have to give account to him who is ready to judge the living and the dead. (1 Peter 4:1-5)

Dear sis, you're gorgeous whether you're wearing a crop top or a huge t-shirt. One doesn't make you more beautiful than the other. Ask yourself why you feel the need to show your body off in public. Is it because you like the attention from men and/or the envy from women? Do you feel like it is part of your personal style and no one should tell you what to wear? Do you feel it's not hurting anyone if you choose to show cleavage or wear short shorts?

Assess who your clothing reveals that you serve. God or the devil?
Some people say God has better things to worry about than sexuality and what we're wearing. I beg to differ.

You were created for specific purposes which include but aren't limited to glorifying God for all your days and joining the Great Commission of bringing the lost home. Do your clothes cause people to focus on your body? Are people distracted by your outfit rather than your pure and joyful spirit?

Some people will hoot and holler whether you're in a sweat-suit or tight dress. I'm in New York, so I completely get it. It's not so much about what they do, than it is about your intentions. It's about what you're hiding; it's about what you're tapping into when you wear revealing clothes that you don't tap into otherwise. It's about whether you feel better about yourself when a guy can't stop staring at you than you do in the presence of God. Why does a man's lustful approval mean more to you than God's love? God marked you approved through the blood of his son on the cross. Yes, it's that serious.

I'd just like to encourage you to take your perspectives and habits to the cross. If you disagree with me, it's completely fine. But at least see what God has to say, see how He's called you to live—don't be so prideful as to assume you can serve God and live the way you want simultaneously. We must learn to serve God, with the help of God. It's the only way we can do it right and fulfill our purpose on Earth. We need to learn to live for an audience of One. We should dress for the eyes of our King. Obviously, what you do for your future or current husband in private is a different story altogether. But did you notice that we are to bear it all for our husband alone? If you're single, your husband is God (Isaiah 54:5).

Do you have a covenant and pure marriage with him or does He have to share your body—his temple—with everyone on social networks and everyone outside?

Girl Chat

1. What are your convictions as it relates to clothing?
2. Are these your own or alluded to by God?
3. How intentional are you about making sure your entire life points to God?
4. Which scripture stood out to you the most? Why?
5. How has God revealed himself to you in a new way through this chapter?
6. After reading the scriptures, are there any changes you need to make to your wardrobe?
7. How does the Bible differ from what you were taught or what you've come to understand about fashion?

Day 20: Tearing Down those Walls

I am the queen of putting walls up for unreasonable reasons and unreasonable lengths of time. I do it to protect myself from feeling things I don't want to feel and to avoid conversations I don't want to have. Some of it is imaginary, while other times they are legitimate precautions to take.

For example, if I notice that certain people can't handle certain information, I'll make a mental note to never share with them again on those topics. For example, God calls us to trust Him for more than we can do on our own. God calls us to believe all He's prophesied no matter how ridiculous it seems and live from that. Think of Noah and the ark. It hadn't rained in so long that the people deemed him mentally unstable. Yet as the rain fell and the waters rose, I'd bet there wasn't one person who didn't wished they'd listened and would've lived in a way that glorified God.

The problem isn't that I guard my heart. The Bible says to do so and it states that the heart is deceitful above all else. The issue is that I build walls to keep out the wrong things! I build walls to keep out boys I don't plan on dating, family members when they disappoint me, and strangers who God has called me to talk to—when I'm in a rush. I block out different ministries when I'd rather focus on work, and the presence and voice of God when I'm not ready to hear what He has to say. I can feel my Spirit reject Him when He speaks into things that my heart has yet to deal with. I quickly reach for distraction—whether I begin to think about something else, play music, begin opening apps on my phone, or I start a conversation—all the while knowing it'd be best to be silent clay. When our Creator speaks—we should never have "anything" better to do but listen. After all: we exist for, through, and because of Him. How dare we be too busy to receive His instruction or correction? He is perfect in all of His ways, and everything He has to say is of the utmost importance. God does not waste His words. There is purpose in everything He says and there's reason even behind the things He doesn't say. Let us remember His sovereignty, rule, and glory in the scope of our lives. Let us redirect our focus from our little worlds and concerns to eternity. We live for another world.

Let's look at a woman with quite a few walls and guards on her heart. I encourage you to read the entire chapter, however here are a few verses from the New International Version:

When a Samaritan woman came to draw water; Jesus said to her, "Will you give me a drink?" The Samaritan woman said to him, "You are a Jew and I am a Samaritan woman. How can you ask me for a drink?" (For Jews do not associate with Samaritans.) Jesus answered her, "If you knew the gift of God and who it is that asks you for a drink, you would have asked him and he would have given you living water." "Sir," the woman said, "you have nothing to draw with and the well is deep. Where can you get this living water? Jesus answered, "Everyone who drinks this water will be thirsty again, but whoever drinks the water I give them will never thirst. Indeed, the water I give them will become in them a spring of water welling up to eternal life." The woman said to him, "Sir, give me this water so that I won't get thirsty and have to keep coming here to draw water." (John 4:7, 9-11, 13-15)

Yet a time is coming and has now come when the true worshipers will worship the Father in the Spirit and in truth, for they are the kind of worshipers the Father seeks. God is spirit, and his worshipers must worship in the Spirit and in truth." The woman said, "I know that Messiah" (called Christ) "is coming. When he comes, he will explain everything to us." Then Jesus declared, "I, the one speaking to you—I am he." (John 4:23-26)

If you read the entire chapter, you'll see that it is socially unacceptable for Jesus to be speaking to this woman. Samaritans and Jews never spoke to one another. In addition, Jesus was a holy prophet among other things and it was uncustomary for prophets to talk with women, especially knowing that she was committing many sins including but not limited to fornication and co-habitation with a man she wasn't married to. The scripture says she was on man #6 when she encountered Jesus at the well.

This woman may have been defensive as a result of heartbreak after heartbreak, lie after lie, false hopes, crushed dreams, low self-esteem, disconnection from God, lack of the intimacy she truly desired and deserved and so much more! She may have been weary of yet another man making huge promises he likely wouldn't be able to keep just like all the others. This woman probably did not expect to go through 6 men in her lifetime when she began dating the first. We don't expect to get as far from God as we do and we don't expect our heart to become as hardened as it does by life experiences over time. But we stray, and our heart follows suit by hardening against the Word, love, and pursuit of our God. He's perfect and He's never hurt us but it's so easy to blame Him for all He allowed—neglecting to face that our actions and our own sin brought at least some of the pain into our lives. Not one of us is without sin!

The beautiful thing about our God is He knows all we've done *yet His perfect love for us remains constant*. His pursuit of our hearts is undeterred. He knew when He made you that you'd do all the things you've done. That is powerful! I always say if I had the ability to make someone, I'd make someone who'd bring me no trouble, disappointment or heartache. Why would anyone intentionally create a person that they **know for certain** will fail them, disobey them, and even have the audacity to run from them? God's favor is unmerited, His mercy blows my mind, His pursuit moves me to tears, His love is relentless, and His thoughts are way beyond our thoughts. I am so glad God isn't like me! I'm so glad He didn't pass over my name that day just because I'd sin and have my countless boyfriends. He didn't decide to not save me because I gave away time, energy, and affection that belonged to Him alone. He never stopped loving me, even when I stopped loving Him. That's a love I'll never understand but I'm willing to spend the rest of my life, reaching out for it. I ran and sprinted from God's embrace in the past, but now I make it my business to let Him in more daily. Those arms were stretched open on that cross for you and I and they're still open now! Our names were written on the palm of God's hands, and your name was on Jesus' mind as He hung on that cross.

His embrace isn't meant to hurt you but we all know healing hurts. Let God do His job in your life. Your role is to allow Him to tear down those walls you've built. You thought they'd protect you from life, but life seeps in nonetheless. All that those walls do is act as a barrier between you and your Creator. Let Him in! He's not like the men who hurt you, He's not like your family, He's not like the people who claimed to be your friends, and He won't hurt you the way you've hurt yourself. He'll change your life and demonstrate how to love and forgive all those people you just thought of. He'll teach you to love yourself as well; His arms are open—open yours!

Girl Chat

Walls are damaging and they prevent your own healing.

1. Has anything ever burned you to the point where you felt the need to build walls to protect yourself?

2. Have you given that situation over to God?

3. Have you sought and accepted healing from your past?

4. What has God revealed to you either about yourself or about Him from the scriptures above?

5. What areas of your life will you now begin to submit to Him in prayer?

6. How often do you allow God to speak to you while you sit in quiet time – completely silent?

7. Is there anything you've been doing, that this chapter confirmed you should continue doing?

Day 21: Why am I Sowing + Not Reaping?

"God doesn't give us what we can handle. He helps us handle what we're given." – Unknown

This sowing mentality stems from the idea that we're entitled to anything let alone what we've prayed for. It's never a question of whether or not God is able; but when and how He'll bring His own perfect will to pass. It's up to you to align your will with His.

If we can agree that God's grace and favor are unmerited, why do we try to shove our merits in His face? We know we haven't earned His love yet we try to earn His blessings. We try with all our might to storm into His throne room and move the hand of God with our prayers, fasting, serving, and ministry. We carry on as though the things we do to praise Him, could possibly manipulate God into moving in accordance with our timing.

God is not man that He should lie, thus if He's promised something you can rest assured that it will come to pass. In addition, He's not man that He can be convinced, manipulated, blackmailed, coerced or forced into anything whatsoever. He is Lord God Almighty—the God who provides the breath you use to curse Him and the energy you use to try to win a losing battle. You will never out-give or out-bless God. Understand that if you don't have your promise yet, it's not the right timing.

At some point, we have to sit down and let God be God. At some point, we have to get tired of running a show in which we were called to be an audience member. At some point, we have to be gleefully content to serve without peeking at the work of God's hands—trusting that He'll reveal it to us when we're ready. Your husband won't come *because* you begged for him. Your promotion won't come *because* you made such a compelling argument that caused God to change His mind. When you are blessed, it is in accordance with God's power, God's might, God's perfect timing, and God's perfect plan. It's all about what God wants for your life and whether or not you're able to use your blessings to glorify Him. Sometimes it's the case that if we were blessed with what we prayed for right now, we'd idolize it and pour ourselves into that thing or person. God wants to remain first and foremost in our lives. He will not give up on your heart, nor will He allow you to take it from His grasp to give to another mist or earthly thing that'll pass away. Instead of handing your worth from dust to dust, take it and place in the hands of our Everlasting Lord. He knows what to do with your heart and He knows how to guide you and mold you into the woman that can handle what He wants to bless you with. Trust Him.

It was revealed to them that they were not serving themselves but you, when they spoke of the things that have now been told you by those who have preached the gospel to you by the Holy Spirit sent from heaven. Even angels long to look into these things. (1 Peter 1:12)

The scripture above reminds us that we live for others. The prophets who told and preached of Jesus' coming did not do this for themselves, but in order to serve us. God has placed us as humans in positions to hear and see things that even angels haven't been able to see coming. Understand that your role on this Earth is so much larger than whether or not you get all the things you prayed for! It's about whether or not you did all the things God asked you to do, to the best of your ability!

Girl Chat

When you trust God's timing and perfect way of thinking, you are able to see a lot of your stress melt away.

1. Why do you believe you deserve to reap right now?

2. Do you believe you know something God doesn't know about your capability to handle his blessing(s)?

3. Do you believe that God will bring His promises to pass in the perfect timing? Do you believe what God believes (that right now is not the right time for that)?

4. What is it that you feel you're missing out on? Be honest and write it down—you wouldn't be in such a rush if you didn't feel you'd miss out if God didn't move <u>now</u>!

5. Has there ever been a time when God told you to surrender your timing and trust Him? If so, has there been a time where you've obeyed and were pleased by the results?

6. Do you believe that God is in control of your life?

7. Do you believe that God has the perfect plan for your life? (The way to test whether or not you truly do is if you see that nothing He does or allows bothers you! Life happens and you retain your joy because you trust that <u>everything</u> that has/will happen is part of His perfect plan and thus is **good for you.**)

Day 22: Dating: God's Way

The important thing to remember is that doing anything God's way *requires* that you be okay with not doing things your way. It sounds simple but this really is critical to understand as it is from this perspective that we can begin to walk in what God has for us.

What normally happens is: we accept God as our Lord and Savior and we may or may not fully understand what this entails. In my opinion, we don't understand what following God will cost, even if we've been in the church throughout our childhood or seen others follow Him before us. My reasoning behind this is though you know following God may cost something, you have no idea what it will cost *you*. Knowing something is costly is one thing, having to pay the cost is entirely different. This is important is because many, if not all, of us sign up for a dream.

I never could have imagined that accepting God as my Lord would cost half as much as it has! If I could've gotten a glimpse of what it'd mean to follow Him, I likely would've said "no thank you" and raced as fast as possible back to my sin. So far it has 'cost' my pride, my comfort zone, my mother's life, my relationships, some friendships that were really important to me, my stability in my finances, my jobs, quite a few of my plans, and so much more. We'll talk about what I've learned later on in the chapter, however, I'm sure no one would want to experience the cost I've paid and have yet to pay during this walk. I had no idea that I'd officially say yes to Jesus as a college sophomore in August one year and lose my mother December 30th, in the same year.

This has **everything** to do with dating God's way; because doing so requires consistent obedience to every one of His instructions. To follow God means to make a moment-by-moment decision to trust God's plan is better than *all of your plans combined*. When I began to follow God I was excited because I was looking forward to the lights, the stage, the healings, the miracles, the success, the intimacy with my Creator, and the blessings...oh the blessings! I knew that when you followed God with your whole heart, His blessings were unmatched. I knew God was capable of doing more than we could ask or imagine and I signed up to see all He could do! I wanted an all-access pass to God's miracles and goodness. I was excited to see it and have a lot of testimonies to tell my friends and family. I didn't sign up for the storms, the tests, the trials, the brokenness, the stress, the confusion, the pain, the persecution, the isolation, and everything else I've experienced over the past few years. However, these things have brought me to the conclusion that though we don't understand how God's plan is linked to anything, it has more purpose than we know. I've learned we have to trust that everything matters and nothing we have experienced will be wasted.

Dating God's way means to seek His face at every stage. You should be flooding God's throne room with questions and then sitting and waiting for the answer. You should be asking God to prepare you before you go out into the world. You should be asking Him to teach you to guard your heart, how to use discernment in your interactions with men, and to reveal everyone who isn't in His plan for your life where romance is concerned. Don't run around dating anyone who asks. 99% of those men will be here today and gone tomorrow... so why bother?

Decide that you want God's best for you. God can help you do things right the first time around. In addition, it is God's will that you do things right so he'll be more than happy to **help you obey Him.** Sis, if God has promised that He will bring your future husband to you then I believe God will be faithful to do what He's promised. I believe that you have a responsibility to do certain things as you wait.

I believe God's best plan for you includes pursuing God and focusing on His will for your life. What is God revealing to you during your quiet time, at church, and through the sermons you watch? What has He told you to do today? What has He told you to work on this week? Who has He told you to call or pray for? Who do you need to forgive? What immodest clothing do you still need to throw out? What habits do you keep indulging in that do not glorify God? How are you doing with all these things? If God told you to do something earlier today, that thing should've been placed in your calendar if need be. You need to do that before you go to sleep. If necessary set 5 alarms around the time that you need to go to sleep or between 9pm-10pm just to be sure. The alarms are to wake you up or alert you if you're busy to: drop everything and go do what God said. Being obedient to God's will is *that* important.

Why be in a relationship with God, say you love Him, visit His house, ask Him for things and then refuse to make His commands a priority in your life? You were only created for His glory. Each time you neglect to do what He's called you to do, you neglect to do what you were literally purposed to do. In this case, your relationship with God makes no sense and you might as well just serve yourself if you're not going to treat Him like He is your Lord.

It begins with obeying God and being faithful with your current life situation. As time progresses, God adds to your portion of responsibility. Over time, you begin to see how the storms you've endured build Jesus into your character on a day to day basis. Over time, you learn to redirect your focus from your own heart's desires to the heart of God. As you make it a habit of doing so, it becomes easier to desire things that are already somewhat in line with the will of God for your life. Eventually, you begin to desire God's will no matter what it entails. Your prayers go from "Lord I'll serve you if you do such and such", to "I'll serve you all the more if you don't do anything I ask because you're just *worth* serving by yourself." What God has already done for you is more than enough of a reason to serve Him wholeheartedly for the rest of your life.

My dear sister, once you reach this point in your walk, I believe you'll see God move in your life like never before. I cannot guarantee that it is at this point where you'll be introduced to your future husband. Nor do I believe that you should aspire to this level of faith in an effort to make him appear faster. My point is, at this point you really won't care whether or not God answers this prayer, you won't be concerned with the timing, you won't be concerned with what other people think of you, and you will walk in humility understanding that you truly need God for and in everything.

If you're dating someone I would still encourage you to get to this place in your walk with God. Decide to let God lead you. Decide to trust God with your boyfriend or fiancé. Decide that when he does the wrong thing, you will trust God to bring you both back on track. Sit before God and remain silent clay. What I mean by this is, so often we rush into God's presence so ready to pray about the wrongdoing of others (See Day 15) and we neglect to pray for the unveiling of our **own** sin. I've definitely struggled with this in past relationships—where every prayer was "Lord, help him to see what I've been trying to tell him all along". The problem is you think: "when he believes what I believe and does what I tell him, that's when our relationship will go well."

The truth is: when you *both* believe what God believes and do what God has told you to do, the relationship will go just as God has designed it to go. Sometimes even though you do everything that God has told you to, the relationship ends. Some people disobey God left and right and God allows the relationship to stand over time. Minds cannot fathom the will of God and His reasoning behind everything. It isn't our place to understand and rationalize what He's allowed; it's our job to remain obedient. Get up and spend time with your Creator if you want to know how to handle your day to day circumstances the way He would. Love those He's called you to love, and love those who have hurt you if you want to have a heart that mirrors the Father's heart.

Set up accountability between you and a few people so that you leave yourselves open to correction. Filter the correction using the discernment of the Holy Spirit of course, but allow the community God has blessed you with to point things out as they see fit. Sometimes you'll be on the right track and other times you'll need help. It's better to have help available even when you don't need it, than to need it, not have it, and crash. I always say: pride says "I don't need it" whereas humility says "even if I don't need it I'll take it anyway." The purpose of this accountability would be to have people who cover you, pray for you, have both parties best interests at heart and are solely interested in seeing God's will be done. These people aren't in the euphoric emotional state that you two lovebirds are in. **They can call things as they are** as opposed to as they desire them to be. As a third party, it really doesn't matter to them whether or not you two stay together (though they do want you to be happy). The goal of courtship isn't to stay together, get married, or have your first relationship where no one gets hurt. The goal is to actively pursue the will of God with someone else, no matter the outcome.

Remember: the goal of this walk and everything we do is to assess and follow the will of God. You should submit your will under His Lordship; and learn to speak nothing but life (in this way you'll bring your future husband nothing but good all the days of his life). In a courtship: you have an opportunity to learn to trust God, you learn to do this walk with another person, and you learn to trust that God will stand in the gap of both of your shortcomings! You also have the opportunity to see God reveal whether or not you truly believe all the things you said you believed when you were single. You said you believed in purity, well now that there's someone there are you still pure in all of your ways? You said you believed in submission; does he have a hard time sharing anything with you because of your attitude? You said you believed in fellowship; do you constantly try to isolate the two of you so you can be alone?

One thing I've learned is to trust God with your "later." What I mean is I keep in mind that we can't be alone, physical, too intimate, too connected, or too open now as we're in a season that calls us to guard our hearts right now. However, if this man is meant to be my husband we'll be able to do all of that and more *later*. Maybe I can't pour out all the details of my quiet time, how much I love him, all that God is doing in my life etc. because it's too much of a load for a man who isn't my husband, but I can divulge that information after we're married. Sure I can't cuddle with him, I shouldn't flirt the way I really want to, we can't have sleepovers, and right now we have all of these limitations—but one day we won't.

Most importantly, my future husband is so *worth the wait*. If it turns out the guy you're with isn't the one God wants you to marry, you'll be so grateful you didn't give to another man what is his! If it turns out the guy you're with is in fact called to marry you one day, you won't regret all the time you spent honoring him! It will give you such a rich relationship and marriage. It will be a great foundation to build your marriage and future family on. He will know that you trust God, you trust him, you trust God's ability to work things out in your relationship, and that you honor him by not tearing him down. You'll have demonstrated that you believe in him, you love yourself too much to settle, and you love God too much to disobey Him *even with the man you're in love with*. Your future husband will adore that you've chosen God over him and he'll pray that you always do. If you both choose God first and foremost, you'll see that God will reward you by enriching your marriage in ways you've never dreamed.

After all, your husband will love you best when he's consulted your Creator on how best to love you, His daughter. It's so worth it to date God's way sis.

Though one may be overpowered, two can defend themselves. A cord of three strands is not quickly broken. (Ecclesiastes 4:12)

Girl Chat

God has designed our covenant with our spouse or significant other to mirror His covenant with us.

1. Do you have any examples of men and women in your life who have experienced godly courtship?

2. Do you have accountability in your life as a single person (unmarried)?

3. Do you have a mentor who has gone through this process and can guide you? If not, have you prayed for one?

4. What was the most challenging concept for you to accept in this chapter?

5. If you're dating someone, have you been carrying out your relationship in a way that truly honors God?

6. If you're single, how's your current marriage to God going? Does He have all of your focus and are your efforts for love and affection directed at Him alone? See Isaiah 54:5.

7. What can you add to your quiet time prayers to help you more so become a woman after God's heart?

Day 23: Clarity + Forgiveness

During one of the hardest seasons in my life, I cried out to God for clarity. I'd taken His grace for granted and the pain of my own sin was searing. I struggled with more pain than I knew how to handle and I needed God though I'd previously been running from Him. Isn't it funny how that works? We dishonor God and then call on Him to heal the wounds our sin caused. Even more amazing is the fact that when we draw near to God (no matter what we've done), His Word reveals the promise that He'll draw near to us! He'll allow the blood of His son to yet again be sufficient for your forgiveness. He'll come to you not as a judge comes to a guilty criminal but as a Father rescuing a child that needs Him.

In any case, I asked God for clarity. I knew that though I was overwhelmed with pain, God would have an answer for me. I wanted to know the truth about my situation. I didn't want to entertain the screaming voices in my minds. I'd gotten to the point where I didn't want outside influence or speculation, I needed my Father. There's at least one point in your walk where you won't want what anyone has to offer, you'll want God first. I didn't want well-intentioned interpretations of why I was suffering; I wanted the truth from He who is Truth. I knew that if I could see myself and my circumstances the way God saw them; at least I could trust what I was seeing.

I knew that God had a perspective that wouldn't *rescue* me from my circumstance but <u>guide</u> me through it. I read His word searching for answers, I prayed and listened for answers, I read books that challenged me to walk away from my own way of thinking and embrace God's perspective. Most importantly, I repented. I'd grown tired of making promises that I couldn't keep and showing up on Sundays to worship a God I didn't truly love. I was done requiring that I understand before I obey His commands and playing around with salvation. I'd grown tired of my walk merely consisting of freedom from an eternity in hell. I knew if I wanted a real relationship with God; I'd have to do things His way. I realized to get God's plan for your life; you have to follow the steps He's put in place. You're not going to get downtown by traveling uptown. The same is true with following God. You cannot sin your way into His blessings. You cannot will your way into the center of His plan for your life. It takes action and consistent commitment to obedience on your part. There's only one way to heaven and that is the Lord Jesus Christ. You must rely solely on Him to please Him. No one knows the will of God so you must seek Him to find out His will for your life, your current situation, and how you should handle your day today.

That's exactly what I did during my time alone with God. I became painfully transparent. I told Him I didn't know how to love Him and if I was honest, part of me didn't really want to. If I was honest, I wanted to do what I wanted on Earth and then go into heaven. I wanted to become holy once I got there! I wanted to have His will, my way. I wanted to control and manipulate His unconditional love for me. I wanted to turn God into a genie to call upon when I wanted something. Essentially, I wanted God to serve me. I know it's wrong but though I never **said** any of these things, I **demonstrated it with the life I led.**

I was content to be holy on Sundays—better yet Sunday during service. I was content to do "holy things" that glorify Him a few times a week and then turn around and push the limits of sin. Why? I guess it felt good. It felt good to place myself above God. It felt good to do what I wanted and then get blessed on top of that. It felt good to essentially stuff my face with sinful cake throughout the week and sprinkle a few spiritual nutrients in there. It felt good to live in both worlds. It felt good to hold satan's hand with my left hand and hold onto the hem of God's robe with my right hand.

It felt good because the enemy told me what I wanted to hear and God gave me what I needed to live. It's like people who have sex outside of marriage to reach a level of satisfaction outside of covenant, and then press in like nobody's business on Sundays to feel the Holy Spirit in a deep way. People do this every single week and feel no guilt. Or rather they smother the guilt in more sex and convince themselves that it's ok because "Hey, at least they went to church and tithed, right?"

To choose to serve anyone or anything (including yourself) is in direct revolt of God's reign and rule over your life. It's a signal that you'd literally like to battle God for lordship over your own life. At this point I'd released countless signals to God that I could do life without Him, that I only needed Him to wake me up in the morning, that I didn't feel accountable for my actions, that I didn't think He deserved all of me, that I didn't think He deserved my life and so much more. I'd chosen to idolize people, status, lust, the enemy's every suggestion, and thus I lived double and triple lives. I was one person Sunday, another Monday, and yet another Saturday night. I knew I needed a new heart and for God to supernaturally break the ties I'd created with people over the years. I learned that it truly hurt God that I didn't want His perfect will for my life, I didn't feel He deserved my honesty, and that I really thought I could pull one over on Him. In addition, all God has ever done is love me with perfect love. Why on Earth would someone try to deceive the ONLY being that has never wronged them? I'm not sure, but I was acting exactly like satan, Adam, and Eve.

God revealed to me that I should never again get so prideful as to believe that I was exempt from falling from His will. He showed me that I naively thought God-related activities counted as relationship and I had a Pharisee-like mentality. What I mean by this is: I thought if I could just get my good deeds to outweigh the number of bad deeds, everything would balance itself out. I thought I could worship my way out of the weight of my sin. I thought I could Christian blog my way out of that uneasy feeling I kept getting whenever I walked into the house of the Lord. Every Sunday, I promised this coming week would be different. "Lord, this is the week I'll stop half-heartedly serving you and I'll get serious about this walk." This is what I kept promising to God and to anyone who would listen!

God said so clearly, "Imani you cannot appropriately serve me, without my help. Stop trying to fool yourself into believing you'll manage to do my will without first *asking me what it is*. In addition, stop asking me what my will is if you don't plan on doing what needs to be done! Your actions and what you allow reveal the true state of your heart. If you truly desired to serve me, you'd do nothing but serve me and you wouldn't entertain anything or anyone that didn't line up with that desire. In the same way: when my children want to sin they avoid church, good counsel, quiet time, sermons, and anything that might challenge their objective."

When our perception isn't aligned with God's, we idolize whatever is distracting us. A life lived apart from God is one that isn't lived to its fullest potential. Revelation, wisdom, and knowledge don't end because you're not right with God. You inadvertently lead others astray with your secret life. God still has a purpose to fulfill (the Commission) whether or not you're a pure vessel. You might be the only one He can use to reach specific people. But best believe the kingdom you've built for yourself will be crushed by His mighty hand –it's only a matter of time. Just take a look at David, Solomon, Saul, Jonah or anyone and everyone in the Bible who thought they were pulling one over on God.

We're crushed when He reminds us of our size and the frailty of our lives. But we never should've left that place of reverence. We never should've been struggling for His throne and authority over our lives. **That's what sin does.** Because of Jesus' finished work on the cross and tomb we have the opportunity to say "No." Too often we don't use the authority over sin that He's given us because it feels better momentarily to pretend we have His power.

Here are a few scriptures to meditate on that relate to God's clear purpose and plan for our lives.

"Or do you not know wrongdoers will not inherit the kingdom of God? Do not be deceived: Neither the sexually immoral nor idolaters nor adulterers nor men who have sex with men nor thieves nor the greedy nor drunkards nor slanderers nor swindlers will inherit the kingdom of God." (1 Corinthians 6:9-10)

"The acts of the flesh are obvious: sexual immorality, impurity, and debauchery; idolatry and witchcraft; hatred, discord, jealousy, fits of rage, selfish ambition, dissensions, factions and envy; drunkenness, orgies, and the like. I warn you, as I did before, that those who live like this will not inherit the kingdom of God." (Gal 5:19-21)

"Do you not know that your bodies are temples of the Holy Spirit, who is in you, whom you have received from God? You are not your own; you were bought at a price. Therefore honor God with your bodies." (1 Corinthians 6:19-20)

"Do not be deceived: God cannot be mocked. A man reaps what he sows. Whoever sows to please their flesh, from the flesh will reap destruction; whoever sows to please the Spirit, from the Spirit will reap eternal life."(Gal 6:7-8)

"For those who are led by the Spirit of God are the children of God."(Romans 8:14)

"Whoever has my commands and keeps them is the one who loves me. The one who loves me will be loved by my Father, and I too will love them and show myself to them."(John 14:21)

"Those whom I love I rebuke and discipline. So be earnest and repent."(Rev 3:19)

Girl Chat

We have to have deeply rooted faith in Truth. Truth is found in the person of Jesus Christ.

1. Do you pray for understanding more than you pray for the faith to believe without answers?
2. Do you struggle with forgiving anyone? Why?
3. Do you study grace and forgiveness in your quiet time?
4. What hit home the most for you in this chapter?
5. When is the last time you prayed for clarity and waited to hear an answer from God?
6. Are there any areas of your life where God has told you to let go of something/someone and you've refused?
7. Who do your actions reveal you follow—God or idols?

Day 24: Peace + Purity

On this day during my journey toward healing, I really wanted peace. I really wanted God to purge me from my desire for sin, lust, and just all things that weren't of Him. I'd indulged in things I had no business indulging in for far too long. It began to really wear on me and grate my soul. It was so bad that it seeped into my subconscious. It seeped its way into my heart, and attitude, and became pride on steroids. I had the audacity to blame everything that'd happened on other people and on God's unfair way of ruling. I painted myself as the victim of injustice as opposed to the recipient of all the sinful deposits I'd made.

I'd just like to point out that **each time** you willingly and consciously indulge in sin—it results in deposits into your life. Indirect indulgences impact you as well but with those you do what you can to avoid bad influences and then pray God would help you get rid of the sins. The most important thing in that case is to ask God to reveal to you *where those seeds came from* so that you can effectively repent (meaning turn away) from the source of those things. If you have all these things taking root in you, with no idea how they got there, you can't walk away from them because you don't know what you're walking away from. Let's get back to the sin you're aware of—in my opinion this is a huge deal because this is sin that *you actually pursue*. These are things you know you shouldn't do and you literally **make arrangements to continue in secret**. You attempt to deceive both God and people as though God doesn't know what's in your heart before you do. I'd admonish you to immediately quit any lifestyle you're currently leading that is contrary to the Word of God—<u>**His Word in its entirety**</u>. As you read this, your heart may be pounding with conviction. Whatever is coming to mind right now, **quit that thing**. That thing you think "God doesn't care that much about" is something God cares very much about. God created you to live by His design! God created you for His glory and His glory alone so if any area of your life doesn't glorify Him, you are purposely disobeying your Creator. I've done that and the repercussions are not cute, fun, gentle, <u>or worth it</u>.

I had to address that first because *sometimes you are the cause of your own distress*. Often, the reason we don't have peace is because we are trying to serve God with 20% level of commitment. That looks like someone who indulges in things they know they shouldn't, yet they pray every day. They volunteer, they feed the homeless, they love the widows, they care for orphans, they go on missions' trips, they inspire others with their profile or public speaking but their private life is rotten and corroded in sin. No wonder you don't have peace, you are fighting a war against God in private and touting the Bible in public. Double lives breed stress, anxiety, depression, confusion, and an insatiable desire for more of the wrong things to compensate for the growing distance between you and God. The truth is: You were literally designed for relationship with God so your heart gains huge holes every time you take a step further away from Him. The first step toward peace is: choosing to stop running from God and making a vow (that you'll consistently honor) to do your best to remain at His feet. The beautiful thing is that God doesn't want you to be perfect, get yourself together first, figure all of your mess out on your own, or even serve Him well enough to make Him smile. God just wants you to accept adoption into His family and rely on Him. When you truly give your life and heart to God, He will help you. The reason you cannot find lasting peace in this world is because Peace is a person. Peace is God.

But each person is tempted when they are dragged away by their own evil desire and enticed. Then, after desire has conceived, it gives birth to sin; and sin, when it is full grown, gives birth to death. (James 1:14-15)

The scriptures dealing with sin and its repercussions wouldn't convict you so much if you were living the way you were called to. In any case, I cried out to God and asked Him to purify my mind. I prayed he'd help me to get a handle on my dreams, day-dreams, thoughts, and the things I desired prematurely. I wanted all of God's promises immediately and I felt offended that He wasn't coming through. I wanted to have the business, husband, children, ministry, prosperity, and faithful demeanor immediately. Little did I know; I was begging God to give me 6 idols. I couldn't understand why He kept saying to spend time with Him. I couldn't understand why He kept saying "Let me heal you, let me restore your covering, let me teach you, and let me into your heart again." I kept saying "God what are you talking about? I'm fine!" I was bruised and battered spiritually, my heart was shattered, my perspectives were all over the place but I figured if God would just bless me already—everything would be fine.

God revealed to me that contrary to what I believed, I was walking around with gaping holes. My desperation for my God was spilling onto the street, it was oozing from my face but I thought I could run it off. I thought I could *serve* my needs away. I thought I could encourage others and that I could manage to somehow stuff these gaping holes with "spiritual deeds". I just kept feeling God say "Imani, if you'd lay before me you could stop self-medicating. That book won't save you! That boy, ministry, obligation, song, or distraction will all be powerless to save you. You've let this world tear at your virtue-- it can only be healed by the God who created it in the first place. Your heart is crumpled and scattered— you've given it to so many people and things that couldn't handle the responsibility of being God for you. I know how your heart works, I know what your heart needs, and it's killing me that you don't trust me with it! Why would you trust this world that's done nothing but disappoint you? Why would you trust that guy knowing his faith was in himself and not me? Don't you know he couldn't possibly love you the right way? He was running from my love and trying to love you at the same time. You know it's impossible to do that! You knew that and you stayed—in fact you did more than stay, *you pursued him*. You actually *chose to stop* chasing after me and turn around to chase that boy instead. I'm offering you myself again. I know you ran, you lied, you tried to cover up what you were doing, and you were ashamed of loving and standing up for me but I love you anyways. I still want you. I still have a purpose for your life. I still want to bless you. I'm still your Father, I still care about you, and I still want to lead you. Will you let me?"

It's just like God to propose to an unfaithful woman and truly hope she says yes.

My other goals for this day included learning to live from new perspective, healing, calmness that only comes from the Holy Spirit, and acceptance of all that God has allowed. God allowed me to experience all that I prayed for and more—once I was finally ready to ask for it and receive it. I had to grow to *want* to accept what God allowed in my life. It didn't come natural to me. I believe others can relate to that—when people pass away, get sick, lose jobs, lose their homes, or suffer in any way we immediately look at God like "Sir? What the heck are you doing?" To which He responds "I'm glorifying myself through the good and bad in your life." My conversation with God usually ends right there—if I even have the boldness to question Him that day.

But the wisdom that comes from heaven is first of all pure; then peace-loving, considerate, submissive, full of mercy and good fruit, impartial and sincere. Peacemakers who sow in peace reap a harvest of righteousness. (James 3:17-18)

Girl Chat

Wisdom really is your best friend!

1. What stood out to you from Day 24?

2. Do you feel you hold fast to the commands God has given you?

3. How often to you entertain worry, doubt, fear, and/or impure thoughts?

4. Has God revealed anything about yourself to you through this chapter?

5. Do you feel God is calling you back to right relationship with Him? (Will you say yes and set out to do it with His help?)

6. What sin do you find yourself consistently pursuing? What do you believe you'll be missing out on if you cut that thing/person off?

7. What does James 3:13-14 mean to you?

Day 25: Strength + Patience

Sin and any amount of time away from God tend to leave you exhausted and weak. You go from relying on God for strength and thus experiencing supernatural energy to relying on yourself. It's comical when we try to rely on ourselves.

Think about it. You've been alive for however many years now, you have your varied life experiences and your allotted amount of intelligence. You have 24 hours in a day to do all you need to do. You are limited by more than you actually have access to in the natural. What I mean by this is: you probably won't get much from the Bible without revelation from God, you cannot wake up without God sustaining your life, you can't walk unless He gives your muscles the strength, you can only carry but so much before it wears on your heart and mind, and you'll likely naturally choose to carry the wrong things. For example, you'll carry anger, bitterness, brokenness, and a grudge. Every time you see that person you dislike (or heaven forbid they post on social media) you roll your eyes, screenshot it, call 5 friends, creep on their page, and then tell yourself you're over it. Are you really?

We need God sis. You were not meant to be able to do this life without Him. That's why it's so hard when we try! Trying to forgive someone without God's perspective and healing hand on your heart is so hard. If a man cheats on me, breaks my heart, lies to my face, gossips about me, and then turns around and says he wants to give us another try—how on Earth do I navigate all of those emotions? I'll ponder: "Should we have been together in the first place? Why did I not see his lack of honor for me and our relationship? Why did he choose to cheat instead of leave? Why was my heart not worth honoring to him? Why would he lie? Why didn't he trust me enough to know I'd be able to handle the truth? Did he not know me well enough? Why would he say he loves me then turn around and lie to others about me? Why would he trash my reputation and then come back claiming he loves me? And where in the world was God during all of this?"

Sis, I don't have the answer to any of those questions. I'm sure as my friend you'd have a lot to say—possibly something along the lines of that you want to tell him off for me! But honestly so many things happen that just don't make sense. Life gets so messy so fast and you find yourself gasping for air. To me, the craziest thing was always that life never pauses. Life doesn't allow you to just take a month off and then press play again when you're ready to come back. So when life gets hard, we're expected to continue going to work, school, church, meetings and so much more. Even though your life is hard; your kids still need you, your husband/boyfriend still needs you, your friends still need you, your parents still ask you to do things, your siblings still need your help, and God still desires for you to follow him just as fervently as you did before the storm came. How do we handle all of these things, well? The answer is always going to be: Jesus.

A few things I learned on Day 25 were to: wait for God's promises, live for Him not what He can do, deal with others reactions responsibly, and don't let it stick. For you, "it" can mean anything. The idea is that we are casting our burdens onto Jesus so quickly and so often that nothing is around long enough to really get to us.

Girl Chat

I'm grateful for the Spirit of God and the spirit of discernment. Let's take a look at our hearts!

1. How do you demonstrate your strength as a woman?
2. What areas of your life do you feel you're most patient with?
3. What prayers do you get antsy or anxious about?
4. What does the scripture Philippians 4:4-7 mean to you?
5. How has this chapter challenged you?
6. When do you find it most difficult to rejoice?

7. What does the scripture 2 Corinthians 1:3-5 mean to you?

Day 26: Redefining Love + Perspective

It is very important for us to take the time to reassess and redefine what we believe. We continually do what we think is right or acceptable. Your thoughts stem from your perspective and your perspective stems from your experience. My life experience taught me a lot of lessons but I've come to realize many of those lessons came with wrong belief systems. In my own life, I've seen my beliefs flare up and cause me to do all the wrong things when in my heart I want to be holy. God revealed to me that it isn't enough for me to say the salvation prayer and get baptized; I had to give my life, thoughts, heart, and time over to Him. I needed to be willing to allow God to work on my heart and teach me a new way of living. The new way of living is God's way—a way I'd never heard of and a way I couldn't possibly know as I'd been doing my own things for years. I'm so glad that God pursued me, and I'm so glad the Lord is pursuing you right now wherever you find yourself. He is near.

Here are a few of the questions it hurt to ask myself, but were absolutely necessary:
- Is my heart *broken* or dealing with a rough lesson?
- Do I feel like I **need** to be with someone?
- Is this need healthy and appropriate at this time or premature?
- Am I needy or reasonable?
- Am I *comfortable with being single* **knowing** that it gives me time to have a better relationship with God or biding my time until I can be in a relationship again?

You blind guides, filtering out a gnat and gulping down a camel! [Lev. 27:30; Mic. 6:8.] (Matthew 23:24 AMP)

The scripture above brought to mind the following question: What gnats are I focused on and what camels have I swallowed? So often I believe that we can wrap ourselves in the wrong things. We can become obsessed with what so-and-so is doing, why, how, when, how long they've been doing that, whether or not they're ignoring us, whether or not they're talking about us, whether or not they're thinking about us, meanwhile that person couldn't possibly be less concerned about us. Or they may in fact be doing any of the things listed, but their actions don't necessarily warrant a response from you.

One of the perspectives I've grown to have is that God is in control. It sounds simple but the application of this perspective works wonders in every area of your life. I believe we run into trouble because somehow we manage to convince ourselves that we are responsible for everything. We alone are suddenly responsible for convincing that guy to like us, signaling to that girl that she should stay away from him because after all "you're supposed to be his rib", getting that promotion, holding our family together, holding our own lives together, and growing in our relationship with God. We do have a certain level of responsibility in this life but we are not responsible for everything that happens. We are responsible for our actions, thoughts, and beliefs. Those are the only things we are able to control, thus those three things are all we should put our focus and energy into.

I had to realize that if I was being honest, I often fell into the habit of idolizing relationships, marriage, and this idea that my future would begin at the altar. I suppose I got this idea from various movies, music, and relationships I'd seen around me. I just know for certain that since I was a child I'd dreamed and planned little by little for the day that I'd meet my husband. Thus for the duration of my life I'd lived each day holding my breath and wondering if "today would be the day" where the angels would sing, the sun would beam on a handsome man who'd look up, fall in love with me at once, and make my dreams come true. It sounds like a ridiculous concept straight out of Hollywood, (which likely influenced my plans), but this is all I wanted.

As you can imagine, it made dating very difficult. Because my end goal was marriage, it meant that nothing before that point was ever good enough for me. That's a huge problem because <u>everything</u> comes before marriage. I wasn't interested in building friendships, getting to know family, or getting to know the person on a deeper level. I believe one reason for that is I didn't know what I should be looking for. I had no idea that I should be looking to see how he leads, his follow-through, his integrity, if he is a man of his word, his ability to excel not just do the bare minimum, consistency in his relationship with God, how he handled difficulty, how he handled grief, how he handled sadness, what anger looked like for him and so much more. Whenever I dated someone I had two criteria. The two things I looked for were attractiveness and humor.

Those things are nice but they don't pay bills, they don't help us out of tight spots, and they don't say anything about their ability to lead me and our future family. This man can be cute, funny, and broke—not that money is everything but how on Earth will we live without it? He could lack direction, purpose, passion, creativity, work ethic, a deep relationship with God, commitment, drive, innovation, a business mind, success, a proven track record of good decision making, counsel, community, a desire for abstinence and purity, and according to my criteria he'd still be fine with me. In addition, I also lacked all of those things. I desired purity but this desire wasn't rooted in personal conviction. I lacked purpose, direction, and I worked hard for the wrong things. I thought my job description was love, serve, convince, and keep him so we can have children and live in a house. I had no idea how to love the right way because I didn't fully give all of myself to God. I served every man as though he was my god since I didn't feel accountable to the God who created me. I felt it necessary to convince a man to be with me and thus take away every opportunity for him to pursue me and the list goes on.

The interesting thing is I have always been successful. I've always done well in school, I was an A-student, I was driven, I was passionate, and I was full of personality. But none of that mattered in the scheme of being in a relationship.

My grades didn't help me learn to take rejection well. If anything it made relationships tougher because I was so used to excelling in every area of my life. I was so used to being seen as phenomenal that when the guy I was dating had anything to say; I'd get defensive. Simmering in the back of my mind was: I am amazing, look at my 30 certificates—how dare you criticize me? When in reality, whatever he said was likely to help me grow or learn something new. I rejected lessons *because I figured I knew* **enough** to be able to **believe I knew everything**. I was brimming with pride and selfish behavior.

As you can see, I was in desperate need for God to take a scalpel and perform open heart and brain surgery on me. I had warped and disturbing perspectives of people and the world that hindered my ability to live the way God designed for me to live. I wasn't able to experience or find the words to ask for this transformation until I did one very important thing. That thing was to come before God, admit that I was broken (for the first time ever), and confess that I needed His help. I had to find the strength to admit that I was weak and that I was brimming with sin, disobedience, pride, selfishness, among many other things. It was hard and I expected to experience His wrath. Instead I experienced a greater love than I never knew existed. He whispered to me that Jesus took on the full force of God's wrath on the cross that I might be able to experience love, mercy, forgiveness, and ultimately the joy of the Lord.

It was absolutely amazing. It was from sharing those few confessions with God that His presence filled my heart and began to heal those gaping wounds sin had left all over my body and soul. I believe scriptures were very powerful in aiding in my healing and learning processes. However, nothing felt better than feeling God personally lift the weights that caused my tears day after day, little by little, to the point where God had to point out that I was free. I was so full of joy and focused on falling in love with God that I didn't really notice I'd finally stopped crying. He pointed out that my heart, though still fragile, was now His and that the one holding it made all the difference.

This is love: not that we loved God, but that he loved us and sent his Son as an atoning sacrifice for our sins. We love because he first loved us. (1 John 4:10, 19)

I love those who love me, and those who seek me find me. (Proverbs 8:17)

Whoever has my commands and keeps them is the one who loves me. The one who loves me will be loved by my Father, and I too will love them and show myself to them. (John 14:21)

Girl Chat

God is bigger than we can possibly imagine Him being and His love runs deeper than we can comprehend. All of that love is yours right now. God is waiting for the day you'll finally accept it.

1. How do you define love?
2. How often do you seek direction from God?
3. Is the Bible your resource or do you seek people's opinions instead?
4. How has God revealed himself to you in this chapter?
5. When is the last time you admitted and repented for your sins?
6. Do you believe that God loves you? (When you do wrong; do you flinch waiting to feel his wrath?)
7. Do you feel you love the way the Bible calls for us to love? Why or why not?

Day 27: Rest + Trust

I tell you not to worry about your life. Don't worry about having something to eat, drink, or wear. Isn't life more than food or clothing? Look at the birds in the sky! They don't plant or harvest. They don't even store grain in barns. Yet your Father in heaven takes care of them. Aren't you worth more than birds? Can worry make you live longer? Why worry about clothes? Look how the wild flowers grow. They don't work hard to make their clothes. (Matthew 6:25-28 CEV)

Another one of my favorite scriptures when I feel any semblance of anxiety is Matthew 6:31-34. Matthew 6:31-34 says, So do not worry, saying, 'What shall we eat?' or 'What shall we drink?' or 'What shall we wear?' For the pagans run after all these things, and your heavenly Father knows that you need them. But seek first his kingdom and his righteousness, and all these things will be given to you as well. Therefore do not worry about tomorrow, for tomorrow will worry about itself. Each day has enough trouble of its own.

The verse that stands out to me is *"Your heavenly Father knows that you need them."* It truly warmed my heart to read that God already knows what I'm going through. It takes the stress and pressure off of me to find the words to accurately explain my situation. In addition, not only do I not have to pray eloquently—I don't have to worry about the outcome or if God hears me. Healthy communication and understanding foster healthy relationships. Trust and rest tend to be the byproduct of healthy relationship. As soon as I read the verse below, it hit me that I didn't have to remind God of my issues every second because He knew my needs before I even realized what they were. That took a huge load off of my shoulders.

Then I said: "Lord, the God of heaven, the great and awesome God, who keeps his covenant of love with those who love him and keep his commandments, let your ear be attentive and your eyes open to hear the prayer your servant is praying before you before day and night for your servants, the people of Israel.

Remember the instruction you gave your servant Moses, saying, 'If you are unfaithful, I will scatter you among the nations, but if you return to me and obey my commands, then even if your exiled people are at the farthest horizon, I will gather them from there and bring them to the place I have chosen as a dwelling for my Name.' Lord, let your ear be attentive to the prayer of this your servant and to the prayer of your servants who delight in revering your name. Give your servant success today by granting him favor in the presence of this man." I was cupbearer to the king. (Nehemiah 1:5-6, 8-9, 11)

Sometimes we need reminders so here is yours: God is faithful, you can trust Him, you can rest in His presence, He adores you, He knows you, He's always been faithful, and He will forever continue to be faithful. He is God. Faithfulness isn't a part of His character; faithful is synonymous with the name of God. God is as faithful as He is real. You cannot separate God and faithfulness just as you cannot separate God and justice or God and love, or God and power. You cannot be separated from the love of God.

We must learn to redirect and maintain our focus. We must redirect our focus from anything/anyone that isn't God and then keep it there. One excellent way to do this is to rely and immerse ourselves in the Word. The Bible is capable of dividing things up on such an intricate and personal level. It is definitely an amazing resource. Hebrews 4:12 says, 'For the word of God is alive and active. Sharper than any double-edged sword, it penetrates even to dividing soul and spirit, joints and marrow; it judges the thoughts and attitudes of the heart.'

Another gift from God to help us grow in relationship with Him is the Holy Spirit. The Holy Spirit has been the friend I've needed to speak reason to me when no one else would, the Holy Spirit calls me out on things that no one sees, and the Holy Spirit heals the pain I am too hurt to discuss. My life changed the day I accepted the Holy Spirit instead of ignoring and running from it. The Holy Spirit discerns the hearts of men and knows the heart of God. The only way to access the Spirit is by believing who Jesus is; knowing him, and accepting what He did.

But when the set time had fully come, God sent his Son, born of a woman, born under the law, to redeem those under the law, that we might receive adoption to sonship. Because you are his sons, God sent the Spirit of his Son into our hearts, the Spirit who calls out, "Abba, Father." (Gal 4:4-6)

But the Advocate, the Holy Spirit, whom the Father will send in my name, will teach you all things and will remind you of everything I have said to you.(John 14:26)

Peace I leave with you; my peace I give you. I do not give to you as the world gives. Do not let your hearts be troubled and do not be afraid. (John 14:27)

Not only so, but we also glory in our sufferings, because we know that suffering produces perseverance; perseverance, character; and character, hope. And hope does not put us to shame, because God's love has been poured out into our hearts through the Holy Spirit, who has been given to us. You see, at just the right time, when we were still powerless, Christ died for the ungodly. Very rarely will anyone die for a righteous person, though for a good person someone might possible dare to die. But God demonstrates his own love for us in this: While we were still sinners, Christ died for us. (Romans 5:3-8)

One crucial revelation that related to my anxious thoughts is that marriage won't make you any less lonely. You have to settle that with God long before they arrive.

Girl Chat
Rest can seem impossible especially as we get older and gain more responsibility. The Bible says we're capable of all things through Christ!

1. How would you describe rest?

2. How will you challenge yourself starting today to trust God more?

3. What is it that convinces you God won't come through for you?

4. What does Romans 6:6-7 mean to you?

5. Why do you feel the need to strive to overcome what Jesus has already overcome for you on that cross?

6. How often do you set aside time to just rest and sit in God's presence?

7. What has God challenged you to do that you have yet to take him up on?

Day 28: Listening + Watching

It is so easy to be so consumed with chasing God and chasing grace that we completely miss both. One of the most amazing things I've ever heard God say is that He continually sees His children pray safe prayers. We pray for things that we are capable of bringing to pass, or things that aren't big enough to fear missing out on. We passively avoid the level of faith God desires for us to have. A huge reason for this is because somehow we manage to make this walk about us. If we focused on God, God's power, God's faithfulness, God's endless ability, and God's love; we'd view everything differently. This is where listening and watching come into play.

Listening is the process of not only sitting in silence but quieting your mind and soul. One thing I used to often struggle with is keeping myself busy when it was best to be still. Though I may not have said anything out loud, my mind would be racing 160mph. During time of prayer I'd be thinking about people, what happened today, what upset me yesterday, what I want to eat for dinner, what prayers haven't been answered yet and the list goes on. God showed me that it isn't enough to not speak...my mind was a distraction from His voice. I noticed that I even went so far as to hear God begin speaking and then begin thinking to the point where I've crowded out his voice by all these other worries. I'd just like to encourage you that though what you have to say is important; the point of access to our King is to hear from Him. If we wanted to just hear ourselves talk all the time, we wouldn't need relationship with Him for that. We should remember that we are privileged to know and be loved so dearly by God. We should be honored to be invited into His holy presence daily and thus find it necessary to listen to what He has to say. He knows your life from end to beginning...don't you want to ask the author of life about what's going on in this season of your life? It's pointless to pray for direction and not sit down long enough to receive it! Often we can find ourselves yelling, crying, praying, preaching, analyzing and miserable. It's important to realize when we've done enough and when it's time to let God move.

Watching is also crucial as we see in Habakkuk 2. In my own walk I've noticed that I can attribute my belief that God isn't moving to my own actions. It's so important to realign our perspective with God's. We can do this by halting our own process. Amazing things happen when we stop trying to do God's job of orchestrating all the elements of this life. When we stop and take time to notice God at work, often we'll find He's up to a lot more than we thought. God is always at work and He remains on His mission. Though Sarah and Abraham tried to speed up God's promise by bringing Ishmael into the world, God continued on with His original plan of continuing the chosen line through Isaac as promised.

Let us challenge ourselves to put down the pen and the binder of suggestions we have on how God should do His job. We can be so quick to tell God what He should bless us with, why, and when He should get started. We are always ready for God to move the way we want Him to. We can struggle with waiting and watching God move the way He desires. For some reason, though we know better, we still fall into the belief that our plans are better than God's. We can still fall into the notion that we deserve God's position and power….much like satan. We don't desire to revolt necessarily but we do desire to be our own leader. The Bible shows that those two things are in fact one in the same. Let us cast off the sin that so easily ensnares us and press on toward the calling that God has for our lives.

Any relationship that lacks two parties that are able to "listen" will inevitably have tension. There's an amount of value that is ascribed to someone when you take the time to listen to them. When you listen to someone you demonstrate not only their value as a human being, but the value of their words, thoughts, feelings, and your relationship with them. When a teenager thinks they don't need their parent they ignore them, talk over them, and then gossip about how annoying they are to their friends. They demonstrate *by their actions* that they don't respect their parents, the validity of their parents' life experience, and their parents' authority over them as caretakers and leaders. The same is true with God. When you "talk at God" you forfeit your opportunity to glean from his knowledge and experience. You essentially demonstrate that you know enough, so you don't need His direction and correction. Psalm 139:23 says: *Search me, God, and know my heart; test me and know my anxious thoughts. See if there is any offensive way in me, and lead me in the way everlasting.*

This is the attitude we should have with our God. That He has full reign to do all He wishes to do in and through us. We can demonstrate our reverence of Him by listening to what He has to say daily.

Girl Chat
We just covered the importance of listening for the still voice of our incredible God!

1. Do you listen for the voice of God?

2. Does He speak to you audibly, through the Word, or through people?

3. Do you watch for the hand of God moving in your life? Are you aware of your spiritual life?

4. Do you find it hard to focus on God during your quiet time?

5. Do you keep your phone and computer on during quiet time? Have you ever had quiet time without those things?

6. Are you someone who tends to worry or plan everything out? Spend time with someone who is calmer than you and ask how they have their quiet time.

7. What has God revealed to you about himself in this chapter?

Day 29: Purpose + Plan

Remember all that God has spoken. Remember it is His miracle to perform and the purpose of all He allows is to glorify His name. Focus on your part which is to be obedient. Let God take care of everything else!

We complicate our walk when we take things out of the context it was designed for. What I mean by this is God has a purpose and plan for every aspect of this life. He has a plan for your heart, relationship, family, friendships, classes, jobs, goals, dreams, career, and your future family. He has a plan for how to use your past, heal your hurts, change your heart, transform your mind, and everything else you can think of. The way to walk in the fullness of God's design is to walk with Him. Our Creator longs to walk with each of His children hand in hand. It's amazing that He cares so much about whether or not you desire Him. He is holy, He is sovereign, He is perfect, He knows everything, yet He wants your heart.

He created you for specific purposes, to reach certain people, to change lives, and He longs to take you where you'd never be able to go on your own. We must believe that God exists and then we must believe that He has a perfect plan. Believing God has a plan allows us to also believe that each event and interaction has purpose. Believing that all of life is purposeful brings inexplicable joy and a new weight to our decision-making. A desire for God's design automatically draws you closer to Him. Art always draws you to the artist. Nature takes your breath away, people are so interesting, life is full of beautiful little surprises and all of this says something about the vastness and beauty of our God.

God is all about future glory. We see this in Isaiah 54:verses 1 and 4 which say "Sing, barren woman, you who never bore a child; burst into song, shout for joy, you who were never in labor; because more are the children of the desolate woman than of her who has a husband," says the Lord. "Do not be afraid; you will not be put to shame. Do not fear disgrace; you will not be humiliated. You will forget the shame of your youth and remember no more the reproach of your widowhood.

"God is mighty, but despises no one; he is mighty, and firm in his purpose." (Job 36:5)

But I have raised you up for this very purpose, that I might show you my power and that my name might be proclaimed in all the earth. (Exodus 9:16)

But the plans of the Lord stand firm forever, the purposes of his heart through all generations. (Psalm 33:11)

The Lord Almighty has sworn, "Surely, as I have planned, so it will be, and as I have purposed, so it will happen. (Isaiah 14:24)

And we know that in all things God works for the good of those who love him, who have been called according to his purpose. (Romans 8:28)

For it is God who works in you to will and to act in order to fulfill his good purpose. (Philippians 2:13)

In him we were also chosen, having been predestined according to the plan of him who works out everything in conformity with the purpose of his will. (Ephesians 1:11)

Many are the plans in a person's heart, but it is the Lord's purpose that prevails. (Proverbs 19:21)

I make known the end from the beginning, from ancient times, what is still to come. I say, 'My purpose will stand, and I will do all that I please.' (Isaiah 46:10)

So is my word that goes out from my mouth: It will not return to me empty, but will accomplish what I desire and achieve the purpose for which I sent it. (Isaiah 55:10)

Great are your purposes and mighty are your deeds. Your eyes are open to the ways of all mankind; you reward each person according to their conduct and as their deeds deserve. (Jeremiah 32:19)

Girl Chat

1. What purpose do you believe God has for your life?
2. Do you plan everything out or seek God as well?
3. Do you believe God's plan for your life is better than yours? How do you react when He turns your plans upside down?
4. Did any of the scriptures listed touch your heart? How can you apply them to your life?
5. Does God often have to wrench your plan for your life out of your hands because you keep refusing His?
6. Do you have any examples of people in your life who trust God's plan over their own?
7. Do you know that to love God is to trust Him?

Day 30: Fear

Whenever fear grips my heart I write, pray, and post about it. I refuse to let fear silently smother my voice. It already has for so many years. I made a decision to stand up to and utilize the authority God gave us over our emotions. Fear isn't from God nor does it glorify Him. I don't have the time or desire to do anything or entertain anyone that thwarts my heart's cry to glorify God.

If you are someone who struggles with fear or any of the things mentioned in this book; I encourage you to take a week and focus on a different theme each day. I did this and the results are difficult to put in words. In fact, the last seven days of this book are the lessons I learned during that 7 day purposeful period with the Lord.

When fear knocks, it is crucial for us to remember key things. It is critical to understand and believe who God is and that He cares. You need to know that God knows you and your circumstances by name. Anxiety, worry, and fear are not of God. That fear turns into nagging, pressure, and discontentment. It turns into what only sin can turn into (something that distorts perspective, kills, and destroys).

Fear causes us to picture the current state translating over into the next ten years and it horrifies us. Fear is our response to a feeling about a negative event that may or may not happen. The problem with fear is that it tends to be linked to truths. We may have various fears in relationships that link to biblical principles such as being a steward of finances, sexual purity, and being led by God in every way. The fear of these truths not being met is not of God because the bible says each trial will perfect our faith and bring us closer to righteousness.

Our sense of urgency (i.e. "God answer my prayer now") is largely linked to fear. For example, the desire for biblical relationship is godly, but the obsession over it is not of God. Obsession takes God out of the process and says "if I push for it hard enough, it will happen." Fear causes us to put unfair expectations and pressure on others as opposed to the expectancy our faith brings us. As women we must learn to nurture and support others through Christ regardless of the outcome or how long it takes for us to see the results we believe for.

The solution to the trap of fear is to give everything up and over to God. Lift your circumstances and relationships in prayer and leave them in God's hands. Be content with your current portion trusting that God will move on the things you've prayed for at the perfect time—the perfect way—without your help. To trust the people in your life means trusting God to do what you can't see in some future time—without your help. Sometimes a leap of faith means something as simple as staying in what you think is a black hole and choosing to trust that despite what you see; you're right in the palm of God's hands.

Make the most of the moment you are currently in and live for the future (eternity). God can use you now and in the future. Be knowledgeable of your current reality but open to the opportunities God may want to create. The truth is you'll end up right where God wants you to be, detours or no detours. It's up to you whether He'll have to pursue you for your heart…your entire way to heaven or instead lead a willing servant.

Don't waste your time on useless work, mere busywork, [and] the barren pursuits of darkness. Expose these things for the sham they are. It's a scandal when people waste their lives on things they must do in the darkness where no one will see. Rip the cover off those frauds and see how attractive they look in the light of Christ. Wake up from your sleep, Climb out of your coffins; Christ will show you the light! So watch your step. Use your head. Make the most of every chance you get. These are desperate times! (Ephesians 5:11-16 MSG)

For the revelation awaits an appointed time; it speaks of the end and will not prove false. Though it linger, wait for it; it will certainly come and will not delay.

(Habakkuk 2:3)

"Look at the nations and watch— and be utterly amazed. For I am going to do something in your days that you would not believe, even if you were told. (Habakkuk 1:5)

For the earth will be filled with the knowledge of the glory of the Lord as the waters cover the sea. Hab2:14

God repeatedly promises that we can trust Him, His will is going to be carried out in all the Earth, He reigns over all, all things are held together in Him, all of creation had to first pass through His hands, and that He will be glorified in everything. God promises that we can live without fear of the future as we rest and trust in Him. God promises that He is before all things and He will exist from everlasting to everlasting. God promises that He will always be faithful. God promises that in Him is the fullness of life. God assured us the Jesus Christ is the way to light, truth, and abundant life! God has done nothing but pour out His love on us.

Sis, will you believe our Heavenly Father? Will you continue to cringe at this life in fear of all that comes? Don't let the things you have authority over keep you from the heart of the One who loves you with a beyond perfect love!

Girl Chat

The only power fear has over you is the power you give it!

1. Do you fear anything more than you fear God?
2. How do you deal with fear?
3. What scriptures to you use to combat fear?
4. Did anything in this previous chapter stand out to you?

5. What changes will you make to the way you currently live life as a result of your authority in Jesus Christ?

6. How have you experienced your spiritual walk shift as you read this book?

7. Is there anything hindering you from the full embrace of your calling? Cast those things out right now in mighty and powerful name of our Lord Jesus Christ! They will not stand. His blood covered that sis.

Made in the USA
Charleston, SC
23 May 2015